ELVIS
STYLE

ELVIS
STYLE

from zoot suits to jumpsuits

ZOEY GOTO

First published in 2016 by Redshank Books

ISBN 978-0-9930002-2-5

A CIP catalogue record for this book is available from The British Library

Design by Carnegie Book Production

Cover image from Photofest

Printed in the UK by Halstan

Redshank Books
Brunel House
Volunteer Way
Faringdon
Oxfordshire
SN7 7YR

Tel: +44 (0)845 873 3837

www.redshankbooks.co.uk

This book is dedicated to two other men of style – my father John Goto and my husband Craig Passmore. Thank you both for your boundless enthusiasm and support.

Contents

In an image reminiscent of Marlon Brando in the outlaw biker film *The Wild One* (1953), Elvis sits upon his Harley-Davidson bike and looks introspective. Photographer Alfred Wertheimer took the image in 1956 outside Elvis' first home on Audubon Drive, Memphis. While Elvis may look lost in thought, he was actually trying to figure out why the engine wasn't starting. He soon fixed the technicality and took Wertheimer and select fans for rides around the local area.

Elvis in the mid-50s shopping at the Lansky Bros. store on Beale Street. Although the clothier is best known for dressing Presley, their impressive client list has also included B.B. King, Duke Ellington, Count Basie, Isaac Hayes, Johnny Cash and Jerry Lee Lewis. Elvis was a lifelong Lansky customer and was laid to rest wearing a white Lansky tailored suit.

Foreword

'Elvis would rather shop than eat' was the phrase my father, Bernard J. Lansky, would recall frequently. Elvis was a trendsetter and Lansky Bros. was there from the beginning, helping Elvis define his authentic style. Elvis had an attitude and drive to be different. He loved to curl his lips and shake his hips in the mirror while my father flipped his collar and styled him.

My father knew early on that with Elvis' talent and Lansky Bros.' look, Elvis was destined to be a star and fashion icon. Elvis defied the traditional dress standards of the time and pushed boundaries, mixing stripes with patterns and wearing bright colours. In the 1950s my father introduced pink and black into Elvis' wardrobe, at a time when it was considered feminine for a man to wear pastel pink. Elvis took it one step further by also buying a pink Cadillac.

On his numerous shopping trips to Lansky Bros. on Beale Street, Elvis was confident in his style and knew instantly if he liked something. He was also generous to other customers in our shop. If a customer complimented Elvis on something he was trying on, he would buy them a shirt or two.

To this day, we still see customers from around the world walking through our doors wanting to discover Elvis' favourite store and to meet me. They all want to shake the hand that shook the hand that shook the world. They are fascinated that I was the delivery boy who would deliver my father's stylish clothing to Graceland for Elvis to wear.

Fashion is cyclical, so what goes around comes around. Elvis' style is still relevant because there are new generations still discovering his music and influence on style. I hope that dedicated Elvis fans will enjoy the new insights that *Elvis Style* offers, and that Elvis' impact on current fashion can be illuminated for a new generation.

May we all have the Style of Elvis.

Hal J. Lansky

Second Generation owner of Lansky Bros. Clothier to the King,

Memphis

Preface

Elvis Style is a celebration of the innovative style-world of Elvis Presley. As one of the most significant pop icons of the twentieth century, Elvis' impact on the music world has been widely discussed and analysed. It is surprising, however, to discover that Elvis' influence on design and fashion has remained largely overlooked. *Elvis Style* aims to set the record straight, looking not only at the design impact that Elvis made during his lifetime, but also his enduring influence on contemporary design culture – from pop stars and high-end fashion houses to street style. Walking through most major cities, it is hard not to notice the guys and girls channelling their inner-Elvis, with Americana and rockabilly styles being constantly reworked and revived on the streets.

Elvis Style speaks to a number of leading design experts to shed fresh light on Elvis' design choices and influence. These include *Sex & the City* stylist Patricia Fields, Academy-Award-winning costume designer Mark Bridges, Elvis' personal car-customiser George Barris, and Hal Lansky of Lansky Brothers, who kindly provided the foreword.

As I researched this book I became increasingly aware of, and impressed by, Elvis' consistent sense of aesthetic values – not just in the clothes he wore, but also in the houses he bought and furnished, the cars and planes that he had customised, and the meticulous grooming of every last hair on his head. His artistry sprang from, and remained true to, the Southern culture into which he was born, and from which he drew great strength. Researching *Elvis Style* has taken me from an imitation of Graceland in the suburbs of Denmark, to the Deep South, exploring Elvis' favourite restaurants and even staying in the apartment that Elvis lived in as a teenager — where you truly can hear the evocative sounds of Beale Street through Elvis' bedroom window. *Elvis Style* intends to offer an intriguing and insightful journey though the crazy, cool and at times kitsch world of a true megastar.

Elvis making his first recording for RCA in Nashville, 1956.

ONE

'Elvis was very packageable; the name, the hair, the music and the clothes.'

Andy Spade

Elvis Fashion

The Hillbilly Cat – Elvis in the Rockin' Fifties

The year is 1952 and a teenage boy stands on Memphis' Beale Street, gazing intently through the window of Lansky Brothers menswear store. He seems oblivious to the passing crowd, cruising along the street in their fedora hats and sharp suits, or rushing past in overalls, en route to blue-collar jobs. Fragments of music drift downstream from the nearby juke joints but the boy remains focused on the object of his study. Behind the glass, a rainbow of flare-legged, bottom-skimming suits in mohair and silk are displayed next to Panama hats and pegged pants in dazzling pink, crimson and canary yellow. At Lansky Brothers it is always show time, with the stage-worthy styles attracting the local pimps and entertainers like bees to honey.

The Lansky Bros. store on Beale Street, Memphis.

Out of the store steps one of the proprietors, Bernard Lansky, who invites the young man to come in and browse. Bernard's son, Hal Lansky explains that unbeknown to his father, the young man in question was Elvis Presley, a singer on the cusp of fame and fortune. 'Elvis said, "Mr Lansky, I don't have any money. One day I will and I'll come here and buy you out". My dad said "Don't buy me out, just buy from me!" that's what started their historic friendship' laughs Hal. It was one of the defining moments not only in the history of menswear but also in Elvis' life, as Hal observes, 'If Elvis had just worn a white button-down dress shirt, he would be alive today, as he would still be driving a truck'.

By the early 1950s, the Lansky store had evolved into the fashion mecca of the South. 'In 1946 my grandfather loaned my father $125 to get started with the store. When they bought the shop it was a ladies thrift store and my dad walked in and said "This ain't me!" and just threw all the stuff on the street' Hal recalls. The shop found a new lease of life as an army surplus outlet and then when the post-war stock dried up, it reinvented itself as *the* place to find outlandish menswear. 'All the entertainers, choir and church groups would shop here. We offered something different and that's what Elvis was looking for. My dad also loved to dress the windows real bright and I guess that was what caught Elvis' eye' Hal reflects.

The young Elvis was heavily influenced by the styles that he saw on Beale Street in Memphis, Tennessee. At the time, the famous street was home to many second-hand clothing stores and pawnshops, which catered for a largely African-American customer.

With the assistance of Lansky Bros, Elvis started to craft a distinctive new image for himself. With his shy nature but fearless style, the 18-year-old singer famously walked through the door of Memphis' Sun Studio and paid $3.98 plus tax to record two songs onto acetate. The ambitious young man hoped to gain the attention of Sun's owner, Sam Phillips, a man with a reputation for championing innovative rhythm and blues music. Having been granted an introduction, Elvis continued to visit Sun Studio in the hope of professional recording work, but it wasn't until the following year that he was asked to join guitarist Scotty Moore and bass player Bill Black in a session that would produce the hit song *That's All Right Mama*. 'I was an overnight sensation. A year after they heard me the first time, they called me back' Elvis later joked. He was soon playing to full stadiums across America and urgently needed a wardrobe worthy of the fans' adoration.

Although Elvis never worked with a fashion stylist, he would gratefully take advice from the designers who dressed him. Bernard Lansky of Lansky Brothers is said to have been the first person to turn up his collar, a look that became one of Elvis' trademarks. 'I would treat him like a baby' Bernard recalled. 'Put clothes on him. Stand him in front of the mirror. And I would say "Elvis this is what you want, right here"…and he would start laughing and then buy it'.

From the outset, Elvis was considered by many to pose a threat to the moral wellbeing of his young, adoring fans. In 1956, the editor of a Catholic newspaper wrote to the Director of the FBI, J. Edgar Hoover, to alert him to the danger of Elvis' stage performances, which he compared to a striptease with clothes on.

Elvis and Lansky soon developed an informal arrangement whereby the performer was given credit and clothing in return for exposure for the store. 'Every time Elvis went somewhere he'd tell them "I got my clothes at Lansky, on famous Beale Street". Elvis was very loyal and like a good will ambassador' says Hal. It was an early example of celebrity endorsement; a system now engrained in our contemporary culture whereby stars are given clothing, or even paid, to wear a certain designer and be associated with them in the media. In September 1956, Bernard Lansky and his brother Guy donated the tweed jacket in bison check and black pegged pants that Elvis wore for his first appearance on *The Ed Sullivan Show*, and it paid off. Sixty million viewers tuned in to see the fresh-faced boy, with the brown quiff, gyrate his way through hits including *Ready Teddy* and *Hound Dog*, accompanied by the shrill screams of the audience. 'It shocked me when I saw him' Bernard Lansky later recalled, having watched the show on a TV set in the store. 'I thought, Man, this boy is dynamite'.

Elvis and Bernard Lansky at Lansky Bros.
store, Memphis.

Elvis' white suede shoes, which appear in
many of Alfred Wertheimer photos from
1956. The right shoe is half a size bigger
as Elvis was suffering from an ingrown
toenail at the time.

In 1956 the young photojournalist Alfred Wertheimer was assigned to photograph RCA's up and coming artist, Elvis Presley. Over the next two years, Brooklyn-raised Wertheimer spent around ten days in total taking thousands of intimate photos of Presley, both on and off stage. The photographer later commented that Elvis was unique in that he invited closeness, even allowing him to photograph the singer grooming himself in the washroom. This image shows Elvis travelling on a train from New York back to Memphis. On the cusp of international stardom, Elvis was still able to make the journey largely unrecognised.

Keen to forge a visual identity but on a shoestring budget, the young Elvis favoured hand-customised clothing. Endearingly, his grandmother Minnie Mae assisted him by embroidering this Lansky Bros. shirt with a record motif and his initials.

Elvis and Bernard Lansky in the Beale Street store in Memphis. As Elvis' fame grew, the Lansky brothers would often open their shop to him at night so he could browse without being interrupted by his fans. Bernard Lansky and his son Hal would also personally select clothing for Elvis and take it to Graceland for his approval.

This mixture of shock and admiration was a common reaction to Elvis' appearance, which flew in the face of the post-war conservatism. As many Americans attempted to put the chaos and carnage of WWII behind them, they now faced a fresh set of anxieties with the rise of the Cold War era and the paranoia of a communist enemy lurking within their communities. A climate of conformity was created, which was particularly evident within men's fashion and the domination of the Ivy League style. Loose, 'sack suits' from Brooks Brothers were teamed with button down Oxford shirts, club ties, cuffed pants and penny loafers. The look was all about heritage, respectability and allegiance – and comply they did, with 70% of all suits sold in the late 1950s belonging to the Ivy League style.

Within this climate, it took courage to stand apart from the crowd. Elvis' image was seen as antagonistic, as it so skilfully played with gender and racial stereotypes. His fondness for make-up – at which he was so adept he would often apply his girlfriend's mascara – penchant for lace, bubble-gum pink clothing and navel-baring cropped shirts were seen as effeminate and highly suspicious.

Against a backdrop of racial segregation, Elvis was also challenging dress codes and beliefs of the Old South. His wardrobe perfectly mirrored his music by blending together country with rhythm & blues style. Without perhaps even consciously realising it, Elvis' choice of clothing created a cultural exchange that was deeply personal and specific to his Southern roots. From a young age Elvis had idolised country performers such as Mississippi Slim, who lived up to the cowboy persona with a wardrobe that featured shirts with embroidered yokes and arrowheads, shiny belt buckles, tassels, and Western neckties. It was a style that Elvis would continue to appropriate throughout his career.

Elvis' love for all things Western was evident in his early stage costumes. He wore this distinctive shirt with a brightly coloured embroidered yoke in 1954, joining the Starlite Wranglers (the group included Scotty Moore and Bill Black, who were soon to become Elvis' musicians) to perform at Memphis' Bon Air Club.

Never one to shy away from colour, Elvis accessorised this pink shirt with a pink belt and pink socks. The upturned collar is emphasised with an interwoven black ribbon. 'We like to take credit for putting Elvis in the black and pink colour combination' says Hal Lansky of Lansky Bros. 'Back then "real men" wouldn't wear pink but it soon became a 50s thing, with pink clothing, Cadillacs and flamingo motifs becoming popular'.

Simultaneously, Presley was also taking his style cues from blues men such as B.B. King, a fellow Lansky customer who was fond of bold, plaid jackets with a tuxedo collar and two-tone correspondent shoes. When the West Coast musician Lowell Fulson visited Memphis to play at the Club Handy, Elvis was there to witness his theatrical stage-wear, including brilliant white suits that became illuminated on stage – a tactic that Elvis would later employ during his Vegas era.

Zoot suit wearers displaying their distinctive style on the sidewalk.

The youthful Elvis also experimented with the zoot suit – a sartorial style recognisable for the high-waisted, voluminous trousers that tapered into a tight cuff at the ankle. The coat was long and flared with wide shoulders and lapels, and a large pleat running down the back, often topped off with a wide-brimmed hat or duck's tail hairstyle. Legend has it that the zoot suit originated on Elvis' doorstep, designed by the tailor Louis Lettes, who had a store near Beale Street and would have been dressing the local Memphians. Cab Calloway's performance in the hit musical *Stormy Weather* (1953) in which he emerges from behind the jazz club curtain wearing a splendid pale zoot suit, complete with elongated bow tie and leg chain, helped in gaining a degree of mainstream acceptance. However, a white Southerner wearing clothing associated with ethnic minorities could still be seen as offering up a challenge to authority.

In contrast to other outcasts of the era – Marlon Brando, James Dean or the Beat Poets, who spoke directly of alienation and defiance – the young Presley repeatedly gave press conferences denying his rebellious nature. However, Elvis' stage antics from this period tell a very different story, as a young Roy Orbison describes the awe with which he watched his first Elvis concert in 1955. 'First thing, he came out and spat on stage. In fact he spat out a piece of chewing gum…his diction was real coarse, like a truck driver's…I can't overemphasise how shocking he looked and seemed to me that night'.

Elvis' hair and clothing were central to his recalcitrant image. Joe Casely-Hayford OBE, the influential fashion designer famed for bringing a healthy dose of British anarchy to Savile Row, states that 'within the context of twentieth-century popular culture, Elvis was at the forefront in defining a new anti-establishment visual language. Like many other great rock legends, aside from good looks he knew about the appeal of being an outsider. His early style was the embodiment of sub-culture cool'. Casely-Hayford feels that Elvis' rebellious image in the 1950s continues to resonate, although his influence is more visible on the streets than in the luxury fashion sector. 'Even today, a distilled version of his look has filtered down into the wardrobes of many self-respecting teenage rebels. I would say Elvis's legacy to street style is even greater than his influence on fashion. The "Elvis Style" remains a potent and relevant signifier for certain subcultural groups'.

On stage at the beginning of his career, Elvis' provocative moves caused outrage. Presley's dress during this period skilfully mixed elements of different cultures and previous fashion styles, transforming them into a new and enduring style language.

Elvis rocking the Lansky look during the 1950s.

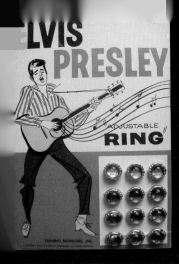

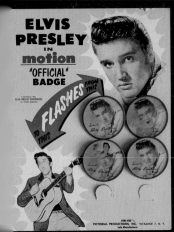

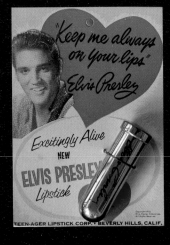

Elvis' style influence reached beyond America. The British Teddy Boys were an early example of a tribe that took their lead from Presley's rock and roll style. The Teds appropriated Elvis' image, personalising it by adding a touch of the English Edwardian dandy. Hair was piled high into a pompadour, draped jackets with velvet collars were teamed with ornate brocade waistcoats and Western style Slim Jim ties were worn with chunky brogues. The teenager, a group previously so often overlooked, was finding its voice and gaining recognition as a consumer group with its own unique tastes, which often contrasted greatly with their parents' values.

Sensing the zeitgeist, the flamboyant Colonel Tom Parker took over Elvis' management and briskly orchestrated a $35,000 contract with RCA Records, a sum that was unheard of in 1955. Accused of a wealth of sins – from exploiting Elvis financially, to hindering the star's creative potential – one thing The Colonel truly understood was the art of getting his client recognised, on a global scale.

In 1956 Colonel Parker entered into a merchandising deal with the Beverly Hills film merchandiser Hank Saperstein. Unsure of the longevity of Elvis' career, Colonel Parker's strategy was to saturate and exploit the market. Lipsticks in 'Hound Dog Orange' and 'Tutti Frutti Red', embroidered denim jeans, bubble gum cards, perfumes, dog tags, sneakers decorated with Elvis' face, teddy bears, record players and toy guitars are just a sample of the avalanche of Presley-endorsed products. By the end of 1956, seventy-eight different Elvis product ranges had brought in $22 million dollars in combined sales – the equivalent to $189 million dollars today. The Colonel even cashed in with the non-believers, by releasing a range of 'I Hate Elvis' badges. Never before had a person been marketed as a product, and the result was that by the end of the decade, Elvis was as instantly recognisable as Mickey Mouse or Coca-Cola.

A sample of Elvis-related memorabilia available in the 1950s.

Andy Spade is considered one of the design world's most creative thinkers, having co-founded the cult fashion brands Jack Spade and Kate Spade, before establishing the multifaceted branding company Partners & Spade. He acknowledges that although stars including Shirley Temple had previously endorsed products such as dolls, Elvis and Colonel Parker were the first to truly exploit the post-war consumer market.

'Elvis was very packageable; the name, the hair, the music and the clothes. The Beatles took his lead and ran with it – all the way to Pierre Cardin, and beyond'. While Elvis may have provided our contemporary marketing template, Spade considers that he also exemplifies the culture for branding overkill. 'Dolls, toys, chocolate; in hindsight it ruined the brands that they stood for. The public gets sick of over-branding and one has to understand when enough is enough, before the fans do. He was the first one to overuse himself. He created the first brand but he also f***** up branding forever. It's so crazy. Shirley Temple never did that. She stayed clean'. Considering the way that Elvis became a brand, Janice Miller, author of the book *Fashion and Music*, agrees with Spade that the 'repetition of images can come to devalue them. I think that was what Warhol was experimenting with in some of his paintings of stars in the 60s, where the repetition of famous faces almost turns them into wallpaper'.

The excessive branding that Spade and Miller recognise, which continued long after Elvis' death, resulted in Presley being considered by many to be a manufactured commodity. However, a distinction can be made between Elvis as a product and the man himself, who in many ways retained more integrity and authority over his music and his image than one might expect in comparison with our contemporary pop stars. In the studio Elvis worked instinctively, exercising his control over his fellow musicians and the music they created in much the same way as a producer might. Without the aid of a fashion stylist, Elvis also had the freedom to use this same intuition to showcase his natural flair for style and showmanship.

Elvis' taste in ostentatious stage-wear was exhibited in 1957 when he sported a sensational gold suit worn for the album cover of *50,000,000 Elvis Fans Can't be Wrong*. The dazzling outfit could be considered a precursor to bling culture, where hip hop stars use flashy clothing and diamond-encrusted jewellery to visually signal that they've hit the big time. Designer Tommy Hilfiger felt that Elvis was 'the first white boy to really bling it up'. He was one of the first performers of any race, Mr Hilfiger added, 'to view himself as being very sexy and masculine but with a certain femininity'. What Elvis' blinding suit lacked in subtlety, it made up for in spectacle, communicating to the world that the poor boy from Tupelo was ready to take his throne as the golden boy of entertainment.

Nudie Cohn, the Ukraine-born American tailor recognised for his expertise with sparkling rhinestones and elaborate embroidery, created the suit, shirt, tie and shoes with little tassels on. Based on a draped tuxedo, the suit was made from 14ct gold lamé and had 10,000 hand-set rhinestones liberally scattered across the lapels, cuffs, pockets and necktie. While the outfit shouts show business, having been inspired by an outfit by the House of Dior that Liberace had worn in Las Vegas, it also manages to incorporate some of Elvis' early fashion trademarks, with the Western style tie and stripe running down the outside seam of the trousers.

Jamie Nudie, Nudie Cohn's granddaughter now runs the family tailoring business in California and feels that the success of the gold suit was due to its shock factor. 'It was so spectacular and just not the kind of outfit people were used to seeing Elvis in. Previous to this, Elvis had been wearing dress-slacks and shirts, so this was suddenly very over the top. Elvis would say in interviews that he didn't like wearing the whole suit as it was uncomfortable to perform in and lamé would flake off of him when he moved across stage' she says. Nudie's Rodeo Tailors became a training ground for a new generation of talented Western wear designers, including Manuel Cuevas and Jaime Castaneda, two legends of the contemporary country fashion scene.

As well as electrifying the fans in his gold Nudie suit, 1957 was also the year that Elvis rocked the big screen in his third film to date, *Jailhouse Rock*. His dance sequence for the film's title track used jack-knife thrusts and stylised convulsions to erotic effect. Dressed as a prison inmate in a fitted striped shirt, denim jacket and drainpipe jeans with thick, white stitching highlighting the seams, Elvis looks every inch the beatnik hipster, shadowed by his gang in their matching uniforms. *Jailhouse Rock* helped to cement denim's onscreen association with youthful rebellion, an affiliation previously evoked by Marlon Brando's portrayal of an outlaw biker, clad in Levi's 501 jeans in *The Wild One* (1953) and James Dean playing the frustrated, suburban teenager in his Lee 101 Riders jeans in *Rebel Without a Cause* (1955). The alliance between denim and delinquency wasn't just a romanticised, Hollywood fabrication – it actually had its roots in the American penitentiary system, which since the 1920s had often clothed its inmates in denim due to its durability and ease of washing.

In his off-screen wardrobe, Elvis tended to avoid denim as it reminded him of work-wear and the poverty of his childhood. However, by endorsing a range of 'Elvis Presley Jeans' for Levi's in 1956, and through his movie wardrobe which included blue jeans in *Love Me Tender* (1956) a Levi's 507 jacket and jean combo in *Loving You* (1957) and the black denim *Jailhouse Rock* outfit the same year, Elvis had become, in the collective mind at least, the archetypal 1950s denim wearer.

Having spent the early years of his career in razor-sharp Lansky tailoring, perhaps by the time *Jailhouse Rock* was released Elvis had sufficiently distanced himself from his denim dungaree-wearing childhood – therefore, slipping back into jeans held less of a threat to his image. The British culture critic Ted Polhemus notes that by this point in his career, Elvis had 'demonstrated that he was no longer a truck driver, so he is free to remind us of his roots'.

Elvis' gold suit cost $10,000 and Nudie estimated that $9,950 of that price was pure profit. Although the gold ensemble became synonymous with Elvis in the 1950s, it was actually only worn on stage in its entirety twice, although he did team the gold jacket with black trousers for a few performances afterwards, notably in 1961 for his Pearl Harbour benefit concert. Elton John later owned the suit.

Like fellow musician Jerry Lee Lewis, the youthful Elvis injected exotic animal prints into his stagewear. These faux leopard skin shoes, with thick leather soles and heels, were worn by Presley for a performance in 1954 and given to his girlfriend's friend as a souvenir when he came off stage.

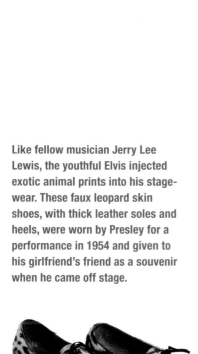

Elvis gets kitted out in denim for his role in *Jailhouse Rock*, 1957. American railway workers had worn this style of denim jacket in the nineteenth century. The loose fit made it ideal for wearing over bib overalls and the denim material offered durability and warmth. The garment has since become such a mainstream fashion item that it is estimated that every American now owns at least one denim jacket.

A photo of Elvis and First Lieutenant Harry Wick at the US Army base Fort Chaffee in Arkansas. Elvis was at Fort Chaffee for just three days, while he was inducted into the army in March 1958. It was at Fort Chaffee he received his famous army haircut.

Elvis wearing the outfit that heralded a new chapter in his life. On 24th March 1958, a date that was christened 'Black Monday' by the fans and media, Elvis was inducted into the army.

Although he wore standard issue army fatigues, Elvis also had his formal dress blues crafted by hand. The German tailor responsible for the outfit Elvis wore to be discharged added four stripes onto the sleeve, indicating that he was a rank above his sergeant position. Elvis joked with reporters that he hoped he wouldn't be sent to jail for the fashion faux pas.

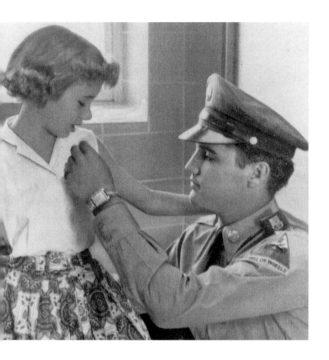

A year after *Jailhouse Rock* was released, they finally tamed the hillbilly cat when he slipped on his standard issue fatigues and enlisted into the army for two years, serving the majority of his time in Germany. Away from the media glare, the 1950s era may have ended abruptly for Elvis but his style during this time has become his most popular and enduring legacy, perhaps even beyond his music. In a few short years – from his first recording in 1954 to being drafted into the army in 1958 – Elvis changed the way that America dressed and created a style that still reverberates. In recent years, fashion design houses such as Moschino, Saint Laurent and Marc Jacobs have used 1950s Elvis as their muse, sending models down the runways in pastel tailoring and tuxedo pants, with gravity-defying quiffs.

In 2015, British Esquire used an image of Elvis in his *Jailhouse Rock* cable knit sweater on their front cover and commented that early Elvis was responsible for 'youth culture switching from black and white to colour'. Janice Miller from the London College of Fashion, says that it makes perfect sense for the magazine to use 1950s Elvis as their cover-star, as 'this image resonates a lot with men's style right now, partly because it is so wearable and can cross generations. I wonder if this is a kind of memorialisation of the young, beautiful Elvis, and romantic ideals about youth, beauty and music that this image seems to capture, before the addictions that ruined his body and health'.

In 1992 America was given the choice between having the young 1950s Elvis or a more mature Las Vegas version on their postal stamp. 1.2 million people returned their ballots, unanimously voting for the youthful Elvis.

Miller adds that she considers there to be two images of Elvis circulating in the popular imagination – the kitsch, jump-suited Vegas Elvis that many people enjoy with playful irony, and the innocence of the youthful Elvis, which acts to remind us that he was a serious influence on fashion and style early in his career. 'This image of him really embodies a lot of our favourite stories about the "tragic star", taken from us too soon and effectively, I suppose, ruined by the fame and success. It's a good story; a poignant story that reminds us to be careful what we wish for'. Miller feels that for Elvis in particular, his ruin was literally written on his body. 'So remembering the body before the decline is important to the power of this story. Such stories are both real and sad, but also, like it or not, very marketable'. It is the unblemished optimism, combined with just the right amount of governable dissent, that gives 1950s Elvis his perennial style appeal.

Rebel without a Style – Elvis in the 1960s

The Los Angeles wardrobe supervisor Donfeld (also known as Don Feld) oversaw Elvis and Ann-Margret's outfits in *Viva Las Vegas* (1964) and skilfully used the stars' clothing to mirror each other. The subtle style union was particularly apparent in this image where Elvis' collarless, sherbet yellow jacket (made by Sy Devore) looks as if it might have been cut from the same cloth as Ann-Margret's fitted sheath dress. Donfeld also worked on Elvis' outfits for *Wild in the Country* (1961) and *Double Trouble* (1967). He received four Academy Award nominations throughout his career.

Elvis Presley costume sketch by Donfeld for MGM's *Viva Las Vegas*. Elvis wore this outfit in the scene where he sings *What'd I Say* to Ann-Margret. The film was noted for the on and off screen chemistry between the couple.

ELVIS PRESLEY
AS "LUCKY"
VIVA LAS VEGAS
"WHAT'D I SAY? NUMBER
MGM / 1964
GEO SIDNEY / JACK CUMMINGS

The photographers' flashbulbs explode as Nancy Sinatra, just nineteen years of age and resembling a Hitchcock heroine in her hound's tooth check suit, smiles broadly for the cameras as she presents Elvis Presley with a glistening, gold package. It is March 1960 and Elvis has recently returned from army service in Germany. His long journey home to Memphis is punctuated with press conferences, as thousands of fans line the railroad tracks and stations, keen to catch a glimpse of the returning hero. Having joined the army as a Lansky-wearing rockabilly, Elvis has been out of the media glare for two full years and the world waits with curiosity to witness his latest style metamorphosis – this is, after all, the man credited with having changed the way America dressed in the 1950s. Unfortunately, Elvis' standard issue army gear reveals little – perhaps Presley himself is also in the dark about the path his image should take. Fortunately, Sinatra steps in with the gift of two ruffled tuxedo shirts from her father's tailor, Sy Devore, and the unspoken question is somehow answered.

Around Hollywood, Sy Devore was known as the 'Tailor to the Stars', having dressed the tuxedo-clad Rat Pack and created suiting for around 100 movies, including the 1960 film *Ocean's Eleven*. Devore's razor-sharp tailoring, meticulous eye for detail and impressive knowledge of luxury fabrics attracted stars such as Nat King Cole, Sammy Davis Jr. and Frank Sinatra to his Sunset Boulevard store. Elvis would also drop in and buy fifteen suits in one visit, all in the style of the Italian influenced 'Continental Look', which was a popular image for male Hollywood stars at the time. The continental look had a distinctively lean silhouette, with a shorter jacket and slim lapels, teamed with skinny ties and narrow, cuff-less trousers. Cult films such as Fellini's *La Dolce Vita* (1960) and John F. Kennedy's custom-made suits by the Roman tailor Angelo Litrico had helped to introduce the look to a wider audience, offering a stylish alternative to the mass-produced sportswear that had prevailed. Elvis embraced the style both on and off screen and became such a valued customer at Sy Devore's store, that the charismatic tailor kept Presley's suit patterns hidden away in a security box.

Elvis' fedora hat from the 1960s. He bought his extensive collection of headwear from Biltmore Beaver, Resistol, Oleg Cassini and Lansky Brothers in Memphis.

Elvis bought this jacket and a number of other garments from Mr Ray's boutique in Palm Springs during the 1960s. It is remarkably similar to Elvis' wedding jacket, worn to marry Priscilla in 1967. The 8-minute ceremony at the Aladdin hotel Vegas was followed by a $10,000 wedding breakfast, which included lobster, champagne, and Southern fried chicken. Priscilla was just 21 years of age and wore a simple off-the-peg white chiffon dress with a voluminous, tulle veil, secured with a crown of rhinestones, while her thirty-one-year-old groom stole the show in a black brocade tuxedo, with a subtle paisley print that became highlighted under the flashbulbs. The MGM tailor Lambert Marks had covertly created the wedding suit, as the couple were attempting to keep their forthcoming nuptials from the media.

This suave, sartorial style was just one of many personas that Elvis would experiment with during the 1960s, against a constantly shifting backdrop of social change. It was a time when most of the previous decade's idols were struggling to keep their heads above water and remain relevant. Along with many of his contemporaries, Elvis was unprepared for the arrival of the new generation of young rebels. Bob Dylan released his debut album of politically fused folk music in 1962, inspiring a wave of musicians who voiced their discontent with society as the civil rights movement turned violent and the Vietnam conflict intensified. 1964 saw the arrival of The British Invasion when the mop-haired Beatles first appeared on *The Ed Sullivan Show*, opening up the gates for a flood of white, working-class bands from England who were taken seriously by both the youth and the critical establishment. The 'Summer of Love' in 1967 saw the widespread emergence of the hippie counter culture, as young people nailed their political colours to the mast through their dress, with flared jeans, tie-dye, beads and long hair becoming the anti-establishment uniform of the Woodstock-flavoured revolution. Elvis expressed no solidarity towards the movement's ideology, and in fact would later write to President Nixon voicing his concerns regarding the effects of hippie and drug culture on American society.

Within this new climate, had Elvis continued with his dynamic rockabilly act he would have risked becoming a parody of his former self. He had only to look at the stalled careers of his fellow Sun Studio stable-mates such as Johnny Cash, Carl Perkins and Jerry Lee Lewis to see that he urgently needed a new image and strategy. These country and rockabilly artists had been replaced in the popular imagination by Sam Phillips' old roster of black artists – B.B. King, Howlin' Wolf, Junior Parker and Rufus Thomas – as audiences became interested in discovering the roots of Rock and Roll. Rather than meeting this new musical environment head on, Elvis retreated to Hollywood. There he embarked on a relentless filming schedule, often making up to three films per year and selling soundtrack albums off the back of the movies. In many ways it was a remarkably canny strategy, as it kept Elvis in the public eye when he could have so easily faded into obscurity within this unfamiliar terrain.

Although Elvis publicly distanced himself from the hippie movement, many of his interests during the 60s – such as meditation and spiritual searching, were very much in keeping with their ideologies. Elvis took to wearing floor-length, embroidered kaftans in private towards the end of the decade. The middle-eastern garment had become the uniform of choice for Western hippies, helped by the Beatles adopting kaftans and Nehru jackets in 1967.

Even whilst relaxing at Graceland, Elvis maintained a regal aura by wearing a silk smoking jacket around the house. This style of garment has long been associated with debonair gentlemen, including Fred Astaire, who was buried in a smoking jacket. Elvis' Japanese-made jacket features Oriental landscape scenes, created in gold and silver thread.

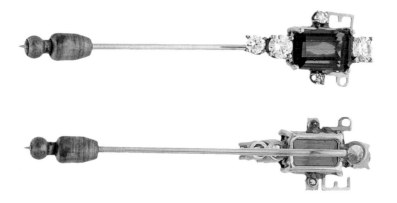

While the sixties were 'swinging', Elvis was busy starring in motion pictures for the leading movie studios, including Paramount, MGM, Universal and Twentieth Century Fox. Presley had made a study of the actor James Dean and aspired to the same brooding, onscreen magnetism. Elvis had already proven to be a master of appropriation and had the potential to be a serious dramatic actor. He also possessed a photographic memory and could remember not only his own lines, but also his co-star's. Unfortunately, however, he was in the right place at the wrong time, as the roles that characterised Hollywood's golden age were rapidly disappearing. Returning from the army, Elvis discovered an industry in crisis as it struggled to compete with the popularity of newly acquired television sets. Tinseltown offered its final hurrah with the 1963 film *Cleopatra*, spending half a million dollars on elaborate costumes alone, but unfortunately it still sank at the box office. Buying costumes from ready-to-wear stores, cutting production budgets and importing foreign films provided a stopgap solution. Within this climate Elvis Presley films became a golden goose, with every one of Elvis' thirty-one movies churning out a profit, regardless of their varying quality.

Elvis' tie pin, featuring a tourmaline central stone surrounded by five diamonds and Elvis' initials. Tie pins were originally used by English aristocrats to secure their cravats in the Victorian era and have recently found favour again, courtesy of the hit television show *Mad Men*. Elvis wore this ornamental pin in the 60s, securing it to his lapel to add a flash of glitz.

Style-wise, Elvis was to become a shape-shifter, delving into the dressing up box that was the Hollywood costume room and trying on different identities for size. Edith Head, the prolific costume designer noted for her extensive work with the director Alfred Hitchcock, worked on nine of Elvis' films, the first of which was *Loving You* in 1957. The self-taught designer, who would win eight Academy Awards throughout her career, was honest about the lack of creative challenge that Elvis' costumes offered and the formulaic approach that she took. 'Basically Elvis wore a uniform in all his films' Head observed, describing the open-fronted shirts that Elvis would wear in casual scenes, and the dark pants, dark shirt and light jacket uniform that he wore for romancing his on-screen love interest. However, if one takes a broad view of the costumes that Elvis wore across the entirety of his 31 films, the characters and styles were reasonably diverse – from a doctor to a racing car driver, Western cowboy, plucky boxer, death-defying lifeguard, singing helicopter pilot, Mississippi riverboat gambler, mixed-race Native American Indian, oil baron and numerous military roles, which served to remind the audience of Elvis' own commitment to the establishment.

A wardrobe continuity sheet from one of Elvis' early films, *King Creole* (1958). The lead role had originally been intended for James Dean, but Elvis stepped in following the actor's untimely death. *King Creole* was produced by Hollywood heavyweight Hal B. Wallis, whose previous credits included *Casablanca* (1942), with costumes overseen by Edith Head.

CHARACTER Danny

SCENES 105 — 113 from 126 Rain cut

Suit
   Coat Blue - w- Red Trim SHIRT
   Vest
   Trousers Dk Gray Mohair Pants

Shirt
   collars Black shoes

Tie Black Sox

Hat Black Belt

Shoes Black - green red scarf

Socks SC 114 Puts on Raincoat

Coat

Gloves Shoes?

Jewelry He wore his own

Miscellaneous boots for the number

CHARACTER Danny

SCENES Sc 127

Suit
   Coat He is back from the
   Vest robbey he puts on
   Trousers

Shirt
   collars Black shirt, then
   Silver trim

Tie puts on Wind breaker

Hat

Shoes to go to hospital

Socks

Coat The scarf is on the

Gloves table

Jewelry Black Belt

Miscellaneous

CHARACTER

SCENES

Suit
   Coat
   Vest
   Trousers

Shirt
   collars

Tie

Hat

Shoes

Socks

Coat

Gloves

Jewelry

Miscellaneous

CHARACTER

SCENES

Suit
   Coat
   Vest
   Trousers

Shirt
   collars

Tie

Hat

Shoes

Socks

Coat

Gloves

Jewelry

Miscellaneous

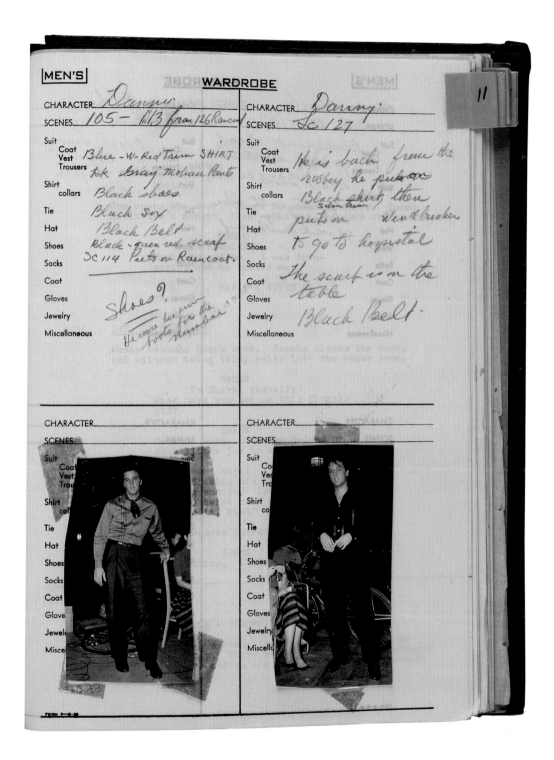

12

CHARACTER *DANNY*

SCENES *#148 THRU 149B*

Suit
Coat *GRAY CHANTAUN*
Vest
Trousers *GRAY CHANTAUN*

Shirt *OFF-WHITE PLEATED*
collars

Tie ~~*Gold Black Bow*~~ *Tie*

Hat *Gold Belt*

Shoes *BLACK*

Socks *BLACK*

Coat

Gloves

Jewelry *In scene 149B*

Miscellaneous *He doesn't wear a tie*

He wears a tie when he does the number

CHARACTER *Charlie*

SCENES *149B. #4*

Suit
Coat *Good suit.*
Vest
Trousers

Shirt *Black suit. (Good)*
collars *absolute shirt*

Tie *Button down*

Hat

Shoes *Black tie with diamond*

Socks *figures*

Coat *Black shoes. Bk. Belt*

Gloves

Jewelry

Miscellaneous

CHARACTER

SCENES

Suit
Coat
Vest
Trousers

Shirt
collars

Tie

Hat

Shoes

Socks

Coat

Gloves

Jewelry

Miscellaneous

CHARACTER

SCENES

Suit
Coat
Vest
Trousers

Shirt
collars

Tie

Hat

Shoes

Socks

Coat

Gloves

Jewelry

Miscellaneous

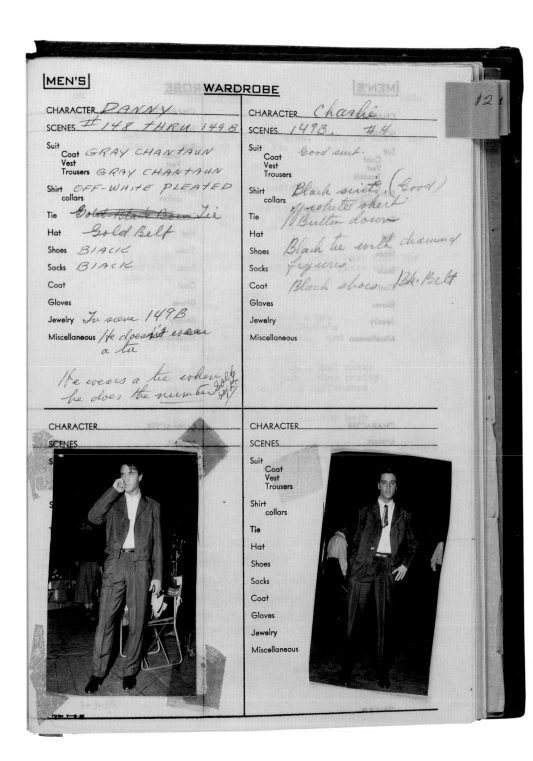

A wardrobe continuity sheet from *King Creole*. Elvis played a high-school student named Danny Fisher, but curiously Presley's photo has been taped to both Danny's and Charlie's character, who was played by Paul Stewart.

Edith Head costume sketch for Elvis in *Fun in Acapulco* (1963). Elvis is depicted wearing the black pants, red cummerbund and white shirt that he wears to sing *El Toro* in the film. The fifth of the nine collaborations between Elvis and producer Hal Wallis, *Fun in Acapulco* features the singer as Mike Windgren, a sailor who loses his job and begins work at an Acapulco resort where he meets his love interest, Margarita Dauphin, played by the gorgeous Ursula Andress.

It was Edith Head who oversaw the costumes for Elvis' most fondly remembered motion picture – the Technicolor kitsch-fest *Blue Hawaii* (1961). With its stunning location, a bevy of attractive female co-stars and a breezy script, *Blue Hawaii* became the definitive Elvis travelogue.

For the *Blue Hawaii* album cover, Elvis wore a red hibiscus print shirt by Alfred Shaheen, the founding father of the Hawaiian fashion industry. According to the academy award winning costume designer Mark Bridges, who has designed the costumes for films including *The Artist*, and *Boogie Nights*, the image of Elvis in his Hawaiian shirt still 'resonates today because it says everything that the film's costume should say. It suggests the far away exotic feeling of Hawaii, the fun and romance of the film, and, technically speaking, the shirt's colour and graphics draw your eye to Elvis'. Bridges observes that this was a technique that Edith Head masterfully used throughout the film, highlighting the leading man in each scene either with vibrant Hawaiian prints or the repeated use of white clothing.

Bridges notes that Hawaii had been made the 50th state of the United States of America only two years before the release of *Blue Hawaii*. 'I think that fact made the locale relevant and interesting to the general public who may have only heard of Hawaii's beauty but were yet to experience it personally. Combining that with the "life imitates art" aspect of Elvis playing a GI just returning home from the army (Elvis himself had just returned from the Army a year earlier) made *Blue Hawaii* a very relevant and unique form of romantic escapism. Today *Blue Hawaii* holds up as a perfectly designed movie and a visual feast from a bygone era'.

Also known as the Aloha shirt, the graphically stylised tops became popular in the US following World War II, as servicemen brought them back from Asia and the Pacific Islands. By the 1950s, the eye-catching Hawaiian shirt symbolised relaxation and leisure-time, becoming the uniform worn by holidaymakers and weekend suburbanites. Shaheen's shirts were considered to be bona fide, having been silk screened on the island rather than relying on imported textiles. He also developed metallic dyes that were used to highlight the decorative prints. The popularity of Alfred Shaheen's garments helped to make the Hawaiian shirt the menswear icon that it remains today.

The Aloha shirt has reappeared onscreen a number of times since Elvis wore it in *Blue Hawaii*. Bridges observes that the more recent film incarnations of the Hawaiian shirt, 'while maybe not directly influenced by Elvis in *Blue Hawaii*, were still chosen by the costume designer to communicate something about place and the character wearing it'. The detective Thomas Magnum wears the shirt in the television series *Magnum PI* to communicate something of his casual Hawaiian lifestyle, while in '*Scarface* the shirt that Tony Montana wears sets him in a tropical climate, while suggesting the aspirations of being a "man of leisure" and Montana's notions of the American Dream. Nicholas Cage's shirt in *Raising Arizona* adds an element of visual noise to the absurd proceedings in the story, while visually setting him apart from his neighbours and the rest of his world. At the same time the graphics of these iconic Hawaiian prints always make you look at that actor, no matter how many other players are in the scene. All of this done, as Edith Head had done, with a simple choice of the perfect printed shirt' Bridges concludes.

Blue Hawaii's commercial success became both a blessing and a curse for Presley, providing a blueprint for future films that became increasingly creatively stifling. 'The problem is, they keep trying to make *GI Blues* and *Blue Hawaii* over and over again, and all they do is move the scenery around a little' Elvis accurately observed.

This image from 1957 shows Alfred
Shaheen's workers hand painting
the *Pua Lani Pareau* print. Shaheen
employed artists and took them on trips
across the Pacific and Asia to inspire
their textile designs for the shirts. The
Pua Lani Pareau textile, along with the
red *Tiare Tapa* print of Elvis' shirt, have
become the most copied Hawaiian prints
in history.

Elvis hits the surf for his role in *Blue
Hawaii*, the first of three films that
he would film on the island. Playfully
offering up fodder for the female erotic
gaze, Elvis spends much of his screen-
time emerging from the sea wearing a
revealing pair of tight white swimming
trunks. More than four decades later, the
actor Daniel Craig would create a media
storm by wearing a remarkably similar
pair of shorts from La Perla for his
performance in *Casino Royale* (2006).

In the 1965 musical comedy *Harum Scarum*, Elvis' character
was styled to resemble the actor Rudolph Valentino, an
image that Elvis become so enamoured with that after
filming wrapped up for the day, he would keep his theatrical
makeup, white harem pants and turban on until bedtime.

Perhaps as a nostalgic nod to his former image, when he had been setting rather than following the trends, Elvis took to wearing this Teddy Boy style jacket in the 1960s. The garment was commonly known as a drape jacket, as it hung from the shoulders and was unfitted at the waist, giving a broad and masculine silhouette. Made from red velvet, with a contrasting black satin lining, cuffs, lapel and trim, the jacket is a fine example of Teddy Boy tailoring, although strangely out of context within the climate of the 1960s Hollywood.

During his time in Hollywood, Elvis was fortunate to have worked with a number of notable costume designers, who saved his onscreen image even when the plots were flimsy, the wigs synthetic and the acting questionable. Leah Rhodes, a Texan designer who had previously worked as both a shop window dresser and Lauren Bacall's costume designer for *The Big Sleep* (1946), kitted Elvis out as a singing rodeo rider in *Tickle Me* (1965). The Oscar winning designer Mary Wills, who also worked on the 1962 version of *Cape Fear,* dressed Elvis for the Civil War drama *Love Me Tender (1956)* while Robert Fuca, costume designer for *The Graduate* (1967) and the television series *Mork & Mindy*, dressed Elvis head-to-toe in Sy Devore threads for *It Happened at the World's Fair (*1963). Nudie Cohn, creator of Elvis' famous gold suit, returned to design a number of Presley's onscreen outfits, including his red and white embroidered cowboy shirt worn in *Loving You* (1957) and the cream 'Millionaire Suit' from *Clambake* (1967), with distinctive black railroad stitching running down the front and along the sleeve. Nudie would later recall that when he made a delivery to the movie set, Elvis would courteously stop whatever he has doing to spend time chatting to the designer.

While a female star might expect her wardrobe to be custom-made, many of Elvis' costumes were in fact bought off the rack. 'This was in keeping with the era,' observes costume designer Deborah Nadoolman Landis, the former president of the Costume Designers Guild. 'In those days, the focus was really on the females and the studio would have a deal with a Hollywood outfitter such as Sy Devore to dress the men and get a credit in the film' she notes.

On 1ˢᵗ May 1967, newly-weds Elvis and Priscilla smile for the cameras before boarding Frank Sinatra's Lear jet. Having married in Las Vegas earlier that day, the couple were about to be whisked away to Palm Springs for a brief honeymoon, which was interrupted by Elvis' *Clambake* filming commitments.

With the task of crafting Presley's image now falling mainly on the shoulders of the costume designers, Elvis channelled his creativity by acting as a personal fashion stylist to those around him. Presley had found a malleable, living doll in his partner Priscilla Beaulieu and the star carefully constructed the appearance of his young girlfriend. The pair dyed their hair in matching shades of jet-black and used lashings of mascara to complement each other. Elvis would also act as the style adviser on their late night shopping sprees. The Presley-finishing-school even extended to asking Priscilla to walk around the house with a book on her head and sending her upstairs to reapply her make-up if it wasn't dramatic enough for mealtimes at Graceland.

Ever conscious of appearances, Elvis also styled his entourage of loyal disciples, who acted both as a buffer between the star and the world and a visual reminder to onlookers of Elvis' prominence. Understanding that his fraternity had an impact on his image, Elvis had his mismatched gang kitted out in coordinating black mohair suits and dark sunglasses, leading to them being named The Memphis Mafia by the press. Elvis and Priscilla also personally designed the TCB logo (Taking Care of Business) that adorned the gold chain medallions bestowed on Elvis' male friends. In contrast, Elvis had TLC (Tender Loving Care) necklaces made up for the women. The jewellers he used to create this logo jewellery included Sol Schwartz in Beverley Hills, Memphian Lowell Hays and Harry Levitch, with whom Elvis had such a close bond that he was one of the lucky few to be invited to the Presley wedding. The TBC necklaces were originally made up in 14k gold but later editions, such as the one given to Sammy Davis Jr. in 1973, were diamond encrusted.

This Swiss-made Mathey-Tissot watch was a precursor to the TCB necklaces that Elvis designed. The watch face is framed by the words Elvis Presley in raised circular letters. The gold, custom-made watches were gifted to Elvis' family, band members and entourage, who could be instantly identifiable as Presley's inner circle.

An example of a TLC (tender loving care) necklace that Elvis gave to his female friends.

A TCB necklace owned by Elvis' hairdresser Larry Geller. Elvis gained much pleasure in giving away jewellery to others. Elvis' jeweller Lowell Hays later recalled a concert in North Carolina where Elvis asked him to set up his case of sparkling jewellery on stage. The King would then cherry-pick items, and, without breaking from his song, hand them out to the females in the front row. At the end of the show, Hays expressed his shock and embarrassment at the expense of the gesture, to which Elvis just laughed and replied that he would just have to sing for an extra five minutes tomorrow night to pay for it.

Elvis' glasses with blue tinted lenses and his TCB logo on the frame.

In the mid-1960s, Elvis developed a passion for horse riding and as with so many of his other obsessions, threw himself wholeheartedly into his latest hobby. Frustrated by his acting career, Elvis sought solace in nature and would start each morning with a horse ride around the grounds. He purchased horses for his entire entourage and their partners, accessorised with the finest saddles and equestrian equipment. In 1967, at the height of Elvis' cowboy fever, he bought a property known as the Circle G Ranch in Horn Lake, Mississippi, to house the team of 18 horses. Elvis, Priscilla and his gang lived at the ranch in a series of cottages and trailers. The commune paradise soon soured when fans began to congregate at the gate, running costs spiralled and the wives and children wanted to return home to normality. This is Elvis' beautifully hand carved leather saddle from the era, which was used at both Graceland and the Circle G Ranch.

Perhaps Elvis' design pursuits throughout the era – constructing do-it-yourself logos, styling his friends and playing dress-up in Hollywood's costumes room, were really creative attempts to wrestle back control of his own image. Without the authority to approve his film's songs, scripts or co-stars, Elvis had found himself in a powerless position. He reflected, somewhat passively, that 'the trouble was, Hollywood just had the wrong image of me – and there was nothing I could do about it'.

However, Elvis' image crisis became an issue that could no longer be ignored. By the mid-sixties, the box office sales were shrinking and even his soundtracks were struggling to gain a foothold in the charts. While Elvis' film career had succeeded in preserving his fame and fortunes, it had also alienated him from the youth culture that he had previously had such a hand in creating. The once radical singer, whose interaction with the audience was now predominantly through his predictable musical comedies, suddenly appeared embarrassingly straight. If Elvis was to retain his iconic image, he now needed to quit Hollywood and return to the public stage as the undefeated champion that he had once been – complete with an unforgettable new stage wardrobe.

An example of an elaborate, embroidered jumpsuit that Elvis wore during the 1970s. The decade encompassed a period of intense creativity for Presley, with a career renaissance and a sensational new image. Sadly, Elvis' personal troubles also dominated during this time.

'Elvis redefined what being sexy meant for men – he made peacocking desirable again'

Edward Sexton, British tailor

The Las Vegas Peacock – Elvis Fashion in the 1970s

Out of the darkness Elvis steps forward, his white suit instantly illuminated under the stage lights. He clutches the microphone between his hands almost as if praying, while behind him the word *Elvis* is emblazoned in red lights. The 1970s had begun early for The King.

Elvis performing during his legendary *'68 Comeback Special*, which marked a turning point in his career.

It is the grand finale of his *'68 Comeback Special* television program and Elvis is giving an emotional rendition of the song *If I Can Dream*, wearing a white, double-breasted frock coat with a deep, single vent flap running down the back of his jacket – a signature of traditional American tailoring – which also allows Elvis to move with ease and to throw his arms wide at the end of the performance. Six buttons run down the centre of the jacket, while slanted front pockets and a nipped-in waist emphasise his broad shoulders. Although the double-breasted jacket can add inches to the torso, the slim-line Elvis with his 32" waist, carries it off with grace. His coordinating, front pleated trousers graze the ankles without a break, creating a pleasing line from the hip to his white leather ankle boots. To complete the look, Elvis wears a deep red scarf in the style of an Apache tie – an accessory that had become synonymous with Country & Western fashion, where a colourful scarf or hanky is secured at the neck with a scarf ring.

As a fashion statement, Elvis' white suit is all about the Deep South. Stepping on stage, Elvis looks every inch the Southern plantation owner, a choice that initially seems incongruous, given that Elvis has borrowed so heavily from black music and is currently on stage singing a song about brothers walking hand in hand. However, look again at his costume and it becomes a sartorial symbol of his success – Elvis has been elevated from his humble sharecropper origins to finally becoming the *Big Boss Man*, as he had been previously singing that evening. In essence, his outfit can be seen as a take on upward social mobility – one of the key factors of the American Dream, which Elvis had long been associated with.

Elvis understood the impact of white stage-wear, using it to ensure that all eyes were constantly on him. This jacket from the early 1970s shares similarities with the *'68 Comeback Special* white suit. Both have wide lapels and high, standing collar. As Elvis wore this jacket for a Las Vegas performance, he added a touch of decadence with gold buttons and flap pockets in reflective lamé fabric.

The white suit itself offers style over practicality and signifies wealth and power. It was the uniform of fallen empires and tragic adventurers such as Howard Hughes and Jay Gatsby. It also speaks of the hope of adoration, as Peter O'Toole discovered shortly after starring in Lawrence of Arabia. Having woken up to overnight fame, he bought a white suit and drove down Sunset Boulevard in a Rolls Royce, 'waving like the Queen Mum. Nobody took any f***ing notice, but I thoroughly enjoyed myself' he recounted. As Elvis stands alone on the dark stage wearing his white tailored suit and singing his impassioned plea for civil rights, he does indeed gain the viewer's adoration, as they witness his career being resurrected before their eyes.

The modern-day dandy Luca Rubinacci, who is third generation of the esteemed Italian tailoring house of Rubinacci, states that this white suit is the best outfit that Elvis ever wore. Rubinacci feels that the success comes from 'the elongated length of the coat, the wide lapels that signalled a move away from the slim lapels of the 60s, and the natural, soft fall of the coat. Although he is often considered an eccentric, Elvis was introducing a smouldering sex appeal into conservative menswear' he notes.

This outfit marks the first time Elvis wore the high, Napoleon-inspired collar, which later became a signature of his jumpsuits and was employed to frame his face. On each wrist is a leather cuff, and curiously, Elvis' left cuff has a watch face integrated into it. Although leather cuffs had been worn by cowboys to protect their wrists for over a century, Elvis' buckled cuffs looked more like a precursor to the leather wristbands worn by punks in the mid-70s.

Elvis' *'68 Comeback Special* jacket and trousers were made from cordovan leather, the thick hide from the rump of a horse which is usually only used to make shoes. Elvis became so sweat-drenched in this rugged material that he had to literally be peeled out of the costume at the end of the performance.

Earlier in the *'68 Comeback Special* performance, Elvis had performed a medley of his early hits while wearing fitted black leather trousers and jacket, with a black low neck t-shirt underneath. The outfit was a nod to Elvis' rebellious 1950s image, but this time a more aggressive, sexual presence was evident. Black leather had long been strongly associated with motorcycle gangs, as illustrated by Marlon Brando in *The Wild One* (1953). In his youth, Elvis had admired Brando and James Dean, but back in the 1950s, Elvis' own rockabilly image and flashy Lansky Brothers clothing had belonged to a very different tribe of rebellion. Aside from owning a couple of leather jackets, Elvis had never been a devoted leather wearer, but given the luxury of revisiting his youthful image, Elvis embellished and reinterpreted history. Up on stage, as Elvis gyrates his way through a string of nostalgic hits, he instantly acquires the toughness and potency that his leather outfit lends.

Look carefully at Elvis' leather outfit though and it differs considerably from Brando's Perfecto motorcycle jacket. Rather than the traditional studded biker jacket, with zippers running across the torso and a belted waist, Elvis' version is essentially a denim jacket shape, but made in leather. This was not accidental – the designer Bill Belew was at the time finding inspiration in the blue jean outfits that the kids on the street were wearing. Knowing that Elvis avoided denim as he associated it with the poverty of his childhood, Belew decided to have a denim jacket and trousers traced and remade in black leather, adding a few touches such as a front seam running down the trousers and hand-stitching the yoke.

Looking at Elvis on stage, dressed head to toe in slim fitting black leather, it is hard to avoid the fact that he looks a little fetishistic. Although leather had started to enter the mainstream, with designers such as Yves Saint Laurent using it in the 60s, it still held strong associations with homosexuality and sadomasochism, butch masculinity and power.

The Japanese-born designer Atsuko Kudo is known as the 'First Lady of Latex' having used the shiny rubber textile to create stage-wear for performers including Lady GaGa, Grace Jones, Rihanna and Beyoncé. She feels that Elvis' leather costume is 'a very powerful male fetishistic look. We all dress for sex appeal and attention, and this look does that in a very major way – he was like a peacock'. The designer acknowledges that as this was Elvis' comeback performance, the pressure was on to 'make a big statement and to dress in a way which empowered him. This outfit did that and became very famous as a result' she observes. Kudo notes that as the outfit is made entirely of leather, it gives the impression of Elvis being 'very animal', yet also manages to be showy and a little camp.

'The *'68 Comeback Special* leather suit has to be my favourite Elvis outfit' says the British fashion designer Joe Casely-Hayford, OBE. 'It became one of the defining images of Rock and Roll. Many years later, I was invited to design all the stage costumes for U2's *Zooropa* and *Achtung Baby* world tours and album covers. I created 'The Fly' outfit for Bono – a black leather trucker's jacket and matching leather pants. Twenty-five years on that look created an equally powerful statement for a new generation of Rock and Roll fans'. Stars such as Suzi Quatro, Robbie Williams, Britney Spears, and more recently Lady GaGa, have also worn interpretations of Elvis' seductive leather suit.

Design sketch by Bill Belew for Elvis' leather *'68 Special* outfit, showing fabric samples of the black leather and silk lining. The sketch has been given to Elvis for approval and he has written 'Ok Elvis' on the bottom left side of the drawing.

Another example of a Bill Belew sketch for the *'68 Special*. This time, Belew has asked his tailor Ciro Ramano to follow the jean suit pattern and line with black silk, using a saddle stitch in silk thread.

Black jean jacket and pants
as per samples

Black
leather

Shining
Black
silk

On
Elvis

Elvis

Bill Belew
1968

Camara—
Make suit in
Black cowboan leather,
pattern jean suit as
Elvis suit in Black
silk, saddle stitch in
silk Thank.

"Elvis Special"
Bill Belew
1968

A V-neck, puffed sleeve stage costume that Elvis wore in 1975 and 1976.

The *'68 Comeback Special* is essentially when the 1970s starts for Elvis. Having become liberated from the movie treadmill and the wardrobe supervisors, the outfits that Elvis wears for the performance are forerunners for the unadulterated theatricality of his later image. The show also marked the first time that Elvis had been dressed by the fashion designer Bill Belew, who went on to create the majority of Elvis' clothing until his death in 1977. By this point in his career, Elvis could easily have had his pick of the most exclusive European fashion houses or Savile Row's finest tailors. Giorgio Armani, Italy's most successful designer, later spoke of his unfulfilled wish to have dressed The King. Yet, Elvis faithfully stuck with Belew for almost a decade, the most likely reason being that Belew was a fellow Southerner and Presley preferred not to cast his net too wide.

Elvis gave these fantastically egocentric jeans to his girlfriend Linda Thompson in the 1970s. Their names run down the front of each flared leg in rhinestone studs, and the back pockets are branded with Elvis' TCB logo.

In the early Vegas years Elvis favoured two-piece separates, but these gradually morphed into the iconic all-in-one jumpsuit that Elvis became famed for wearing. This two-piece stage costume was made from white deerskin, embellished with a hand-painted floral pattern. Velcro was used to secure the side seams and cuffs. The outfit was part of a group of eight costumes that were custom made for Elvis in the 1970s by North Beach Leathers.

Elvis' fluctuating weight meant that his jewellery didn't always fit him. This oval blue gem ring was handed to a member of Elvis' entourage after it almost fell off his finger on stage in the early 1970s. Elvis later told his friend to keep the ring, which is set in a square of 14k gold and inscribed with Elvis' initials.

Part of Elvis' stage act in the 1970s was to theatrically throw silk scarves out into the audience, often with his signature stamped in the corner. An Elvis concert scarf became particularly treasured if the star had used it to wipe the perspiration from his brow, before bestowing it upon a fan. Elvis even had an on-stage 'scarf man', whose job involved placing a fresh scarf around Presley's neck each time he flung one into the front row.

Elvis' rubellite ring from the early 1970s. The stone is a large synthetic ruby, encased in a 9k gold setting. Wearing a rubellite gemstone is traditionally believed to strengthen devotional love. Elvis later gave the ring to his girlfriend Linda Thompson, who apparently sold it to a store in Beverly Hills; along with most of jewellery that Presley had given her.

Elvis' striking 14k yellow gold ring with a single diamond and a large black star sapphire. The Memphis jeweller Lowell Hays was invited out on tour with Elvis during the 1970s, taking a suitcase full of gems so Presley could get his jewellery fix while away from home. Hays sold this ring to Elvis while he was performing in Ashville, North Carolina.

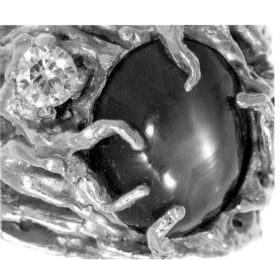

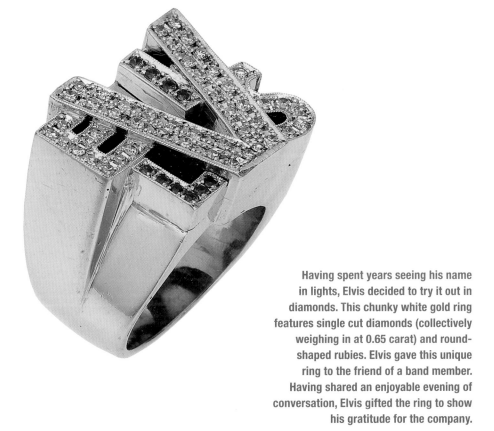

Having spent years seeing his name in lights, Elvis decided to try it out in diamonds. This chunky white gold ring features single cut diamonds (collectively weighing in at 0.65 carat) and round-shaped rubies. Elvis gave this unique ring to the friend of a band member. Having shared an enjoyable evening of conversation, Elvis gifted the ring to show his gratitude for the company.

Following the success of the *'68 Comeback Special*, Elvis returned to live performing with a bang, and by 1970 had become the most successful act that Las Vegas had ever witnessed. Elvis and Sin City were soon to become synonymous, as the performer Beyoncé acknowledges, 'When you think of Vegas, you think of Elvis; you think of show business; you think of flash'. 1970 was also the year that Elvis started incorporating the legendary jumpsuit into his stage wardrobe. Although the first ever jumpsuit is often attributed to the Italian artist Thayaht in 1917, his loose fitting design shares a closer DNA with the boiler suit, now worn by manual labourers. As a women's fashion item, the jumpsuit has fallen in and out of favour since the 1930s, becoming popular in the sci-fi loving 60s when designers such as Courreges were reimagining it in whipcord and organza.

Elvis' early jumpsuits had a simple silhouette and were often embellished with exaggerated bead fringing, which was later trimmed down as it became hazardous when Elvis got caught up in it on stage. Tasselled belts made from macramé, a popular technique at the time of knotting textiles, were added and constantly interchanged to refresh the Elvis' stage costumes for each performance. These early suits often featured a fitted point sleeve – a feature popular with traditional wedding dresses. Silver metal concho rings, originally used to decorate cowboy's saddles, were also used as embellishment.

Elvis' distinctive nylon shirt was from Nik Nik – an Italian brand that became popular for their gaudy, disco shirts in the 1970s.

Bill Belew, who designed around 75 jumpsuits in total for Elvis, explained the design of Elvis' jumpsuits as a logical progression from karate training uniform to one-piece apparel, which allowed the entertainer to move freely on stage. Although this may be valid, there was still something slightly left field about Elvis suddenly embracing the jumpsuit.

Yet in many ways Elvis' entire 1970s wardrobe, including his jumpsuits, can be seen as rooted in the culture of Western wear – a style of clothing that derives from the myth of the nineteenth-century American West. Singing cowboys such as Gene Autry and Roy Rogers were wearing skin-tight, rodeo style outfits in the 1930s and 40s that share an affinity with Elvis' Vegas costumes. Elvin Sweeten, from the Gene Autry Museum in Oklahoma, says that although it may look as if Autry was wearing a one-piece garment, it was actually a western shirt and separate trousers. He is keen to point out that the Western style of clothing that Autry wore was for the benefit of public appearances, rather than clothing that a working cowboy might wear – a fact that ties in with the romantic aura of Wild West fashion, which offers an idealised American legacy.

An early example of Elvis' legendary Las Vegas stage-wear. This 'Concho Jumpsuit' was named after the silver rings that embellish the costume, running down the back of the arms, the outside leg seams and the collar. Elvis wore this jumpsuit on stage in Las Vegas during the filming of the 1970 documentary *Elvis: That's The Way It Is*, a Golden Globe Award-winning documentary that Martin Scorsese had worked on.

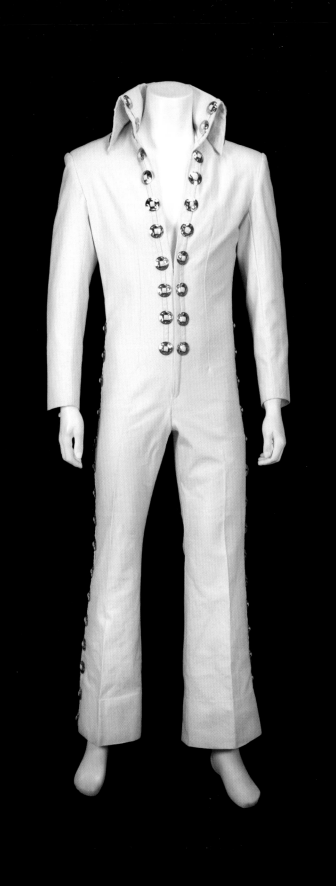

The liberal use of sparkling rock rhinestones, heavy embroidery, exaggerated fringing and oversized belt buckles that Elvis wore are all identifiable as features of Western wear. In 1971, Elvis even started wearing a style of two-piece suits and jumpsuits that he called the 'Cisco Kid', as the studded leather yokes in contrasting colours made him look like the fictional cowboy.

Elvis' personal wardrobe retained many of the theatrical elements of his stage-wear. This tan overcoat from the 1970s incorporates a fur capelet and was made by IC Costume Co, Hollywood.

The Indian Feather Suit, worn from 1975–77. The suit featured a low V-neck and intricate embroidery of Native American motifs and feathers.

Tellingly, during the 1970s Belew was designing both Elvis' stage and personal wardrobe. Unlike David Bowie, who used Ziggy Stardust as his on-stage rock-god alter ego, for Elvis it was always show time. Even when relaxing in his Graceland home, Elvis would have his personal hairdresser Larry Geller style his hair each evening, before slipping on a silk puff-sleeved shirt, elasticated at the upper arm and bellbottom pants, and inviting some of the fans at the gate into his home for entertainment. On a personal, impromptu visit to meet President Nixon in 1970, Elvis wore head-to-toe stage gear, coordinating his *'68 Comeback Special* black velvet jacket, with the black tunic and trousers that he had worn on stage in Las Vegas the previous year. In case it was not obvious who the real champion was, Elvis completed the look with a gold belt that had been awarded for breaking Las Vegas attendance records.

Elvis meets President Nixon on 21st December 1970. Elvis arrived at the White House with a Colt .45 pistol as a gift for Nixon. 'You dress kind of strange, don't you?' the president was reported to have remarked to Elvis. 'Well, Mr President, you got your show and I got mine' Elvis replied. Nixon was persuaded to honour the singer with a badge from the Federal Bureau of Narcotics and Dangerous Drugs. Elvis believed that the badge would give him the power to travel globally while carrying drugs and guns.

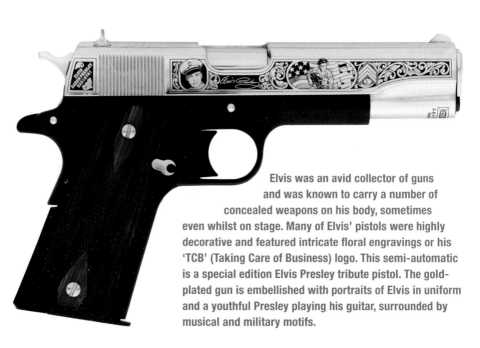

Elvis was an avid collector of guns and was known to carry a number of concealed weapons on his body, sometimes even whilst on stage. Many of Elvis' pistols were highly decorative and featured intricate floral engravings or his 'TCB' (Taking Care of Business) logo. This semi-automatic is a special edition Elvis Presley tribute pistol. The gold-plated gun is embellished with portraits of Elvis in uniform and a youthful Presley playing his guitar, surrounded by musical and military motifs.

Elvis had a fascination with law enforcement and from the mid-1960s onwards, built up a substantial collection of related paraphernalia, including police uniforms and badges. His longstanding interest in the emergency services started when he was a teenager and would hang around his local Memphis fire station, attracted by the sense of risk and camaraderie that he felt must exist within the forces. As his fame grew, Elvis soon needed almost constant security and he became friendly with officers from a number of state police departments. Elvis would make donations to his local police forces, shower the local officers with expensive jewellery and even gifted a Mercedes Benz to the Shelby County Sheriff. Presley was given many honorary titles, including Memphis Police department's Special Deputy Sheriff. On at least one occasion, Elvis attended the scene of an automobile accident, flashed his police badge and tended to the victims.

Elvis' gold-painted hunting knife, with a handle moulded into the shape of a naked woman. On the right is the leather sheath with metal tip.

In 1971 Elvis started to wear capes, often lined in a bright silk so he resembled a matador in action. Elvis admitted that as a child he would imagine himself as the hero of his comic books, and now he was able to indulge his caped crusader fantasies every night before the high-rolling Vegas crowd, or in front of hordes of appreciative fans who packed the stadiums as he relentlessly toured across America, performing at over 1,000 concerts during the 1970s. The capes were attached with Velcro or hook and eyes, so Elvis could easily remove them and throw them into the crowd. By the end of 1973, the capes had been phased out and replaced with intricate embroidery work, often depicting predators such as tigers or eagles.

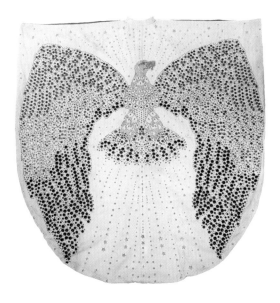

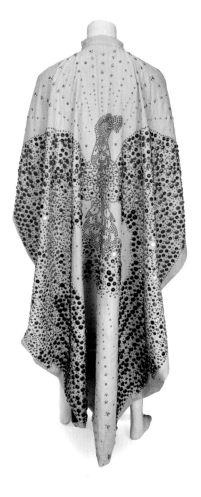

Elvis' original *Aloha from Hawaii* cape. This floor-length cape was intended to be worn for the opening of the televised concert in 1973. Unfortunately it was too heavy, so the designer Bill Belew hastily created a shorter version that Elvis wore instead, and romanced the fans by throwing it into the audience at the end of the show. This version of the cape uses red, white, blue and gold studs to create the image of an American eagle and is lined in blue satin.

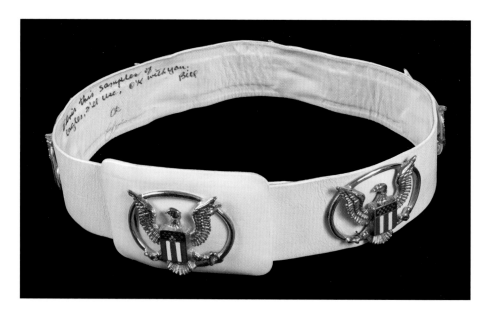

Elvis loved elaborate accessories, such as this belt that combines six gold bald eagles with the American flag. This is a prototype of the white leather belt that Elvis wore during the *Aloha from Hawaii* concert. It includes a handwritten message from Bill Belew saying "Elvis this sample of eagles I'll use. Ok with you." Elvis wrote in response "Ok Elvis".

Reviewing an Elvis concert in 1972 for the *New York Times*, Chris Chase said that 'Elvis appeared, materialized, in a white suit of lights, shining with golden appliqués, the shirt front slashed to show his chest'. Around his shoulders was a 'cape lined in a cloth of gold, its collar faced with scarlet. It was anything you wanted to call it, gaudy, vulgar, magnificent'. Working on instinct, the designer Bill Belew would stand in the crowd to gauge the reaction to his creations – it was through the fans' encouragement that he became ever more audacious and spectacular, creating outfits where embroidery flames would quite literally be licking Elvis' body, or a firework display of studs would explode across his jumpsuits and capes. For the 1973 *Aloha from Hawaii* satellite broadcast, watched by over 1 billion viewers, Elvis wore a patriotic white jumpsuit with a heavily jewelled American eagle on the front, back and cape and a belt embellished with stars and eagles – a show-stopping outfit that cost $65,000 to make.

'The flamboyance of Elvis' stage-wear liberated men to wear clothes that were more outrageous than men had worn since the nineteenth century' acknowledges Edward Sexton, the British tailor who rejuvenated Savile Row in the late 60s, attracting a heady mix of aristocrats and show-business stars that included The Beatles and The Rolling Stones. 'Elvis redefined what being sexy meant for men – he made peacocking desirable again'.

To be sexual, provocative and a little effeminate became accepted on both sides of the Atlantic, with young men rejecting the orthodoxies of standardised masculinity and experimenting with clothing previously reserved for women. In 1969, Mick Jagger performed at Hyde Park wearing a delicate white dress designed by Michael Fish, somehow leaving the stage every inch the virile male. According to the fashion historian Geoffrey Aquilina Ross, the flamboyance of menswear during this time acted as a heterosexual mating call. 'Like the strutting peacock with his eye-catching tail plumage, this extravagance was a way of signalling presence and availability to the opposite sex'.

In an era when men were starting to occupy the erotic gaze, Elvis' revealing, body-accentuating jumpsuits fell very much within the seductive fashion zeitgeist. It is perhaps because Elvis' own machismo had been so firmly established previously, that he was confident displaying his jump-suited body in this way, without his sexuality being brought into question. Bill Belew, who had also designed for female performers such as Josephine Baker and Ella Fitzgerald, stated that while he wanted Elvis' clothing to be seductive, 'I never wanted anything to compromise his masculinity.'

A hot pink jumpsuit made for Elvis by
the legendary rodeo tailor Nudie Cohn.
The costume is decorated with hand-
sewn jewels and rhinestones.

The Red Phoenix Suit, worn on stage in Las Vegas in 1974 and 1975. In Elvis' final years, his stage-wear often took centre stage and created a spectacle when his performances became unpredictable.

Victoria Broackes is the Head of Theatre and Performance Exhibitions at London's Victoria & Albert Museum. She co-curated the hugely popular *David Bowie Is* exhibition at the V&A in 2013, and acknowledges a synergy between the British glam rock legend and Elvis Presley. 'They are of course both known for their famous jumpsuits – although Bowie's were in fact catsuits'. Broackes feels that during the 1970s both performers were looking towards Asia for style inspiration.

'Elvis' suits, while iconic and style-defining, were actually created for their functionality' Broackes observes. 'Elvis was a black belt in karate, and wanted to incorporate karate moves into his performance: the jumpsuit made this possible. Elvis belongs to an era where a narrative in concerts was not required. He was a pure entertainer, who would use all his best assets to please audiences'. Comparatively, Broackes sees Bowie's costumes as 'expressions of theatricality, flamboyance, and sexual ambiguity, taking inspiration from both samurai and kabuki culture. The Japanese designer Kansai Yamamoto's designs for him included a quilted black PVC jumpsuit with vast, rigid flares and a candy-striped spandex body-stocking, as well as various flamboyant kimonos and robes'.

David Bowie wearing a Kansai Yamamoto designed costume entitled 'Rites of Spring', 1973.

This outfit was designed by the IC Costume Company and worn on stage by Elvis in 1975. It is commonly referred to as the Penguin Suit. Elvis had a number of stage costumes in this style, which he also liked to wear off-stage. The two-piece costume included an embroidered built-in jacket belt and Native American style beading.

'While still ostentatious, Elvis' stage costumes were designed to be functional and masculine, while Bowie's were designed to be provocative and outrageous. Each perfectly represent their time and place' Broackes concludes.

From 1974 onwards, Elvis' performances were getting more erratic and started to slip into self-parody, aided by the exorbitance of his stage clothing. Priscilla, his by now ex-wife, acknowledged this when she observed that in his later years, Elvis resorted to sheer flamboyance, 'symbolized by his costumes, each more elaborate than the one before, loaded with an overabundance of fake stones, studs, and fringes. He was performing in garb that added thirty-five pounds to his weight'. She felt Elvis was determined to upstage himself, rather than relying on his natural talent. In the final years of his life, Elvis appeared on stage wearing the 'Totem Pole' suit, a heavily embroidered gypsy costume, complete with peasant shirt and bejewelled choker. Another of his later outfits was a white jumpsuit with a gold Mexican sundial emblazoned across the chest and a belt dripping in gold chains.

One wonders how Elvis could have trumped the pure theatre of these later costumes. Legend has it that Bill Belew was actually working on his most outlandish outfit to date when Elvis died in his Graceland home on 16th August 1977. The 'Laser Suit' was to be covered in hundreds of jewels and rhinestones, so the material shone like a diamond. A laser would then be directed at the larger stones, making Elvis into a mobile laser show. It seems a fitting climax for the performer who had become, quite literally, a one-man-spectacular.

The difficulties that plagued Elvis in later life – his drug dependency, weight gain and ageing body – are not in themselves that unusual or unique in men approaching early middle age. However, what Elvis' wardrobe from the mid-1970s onwards does reveal, is that sadly the performer was in denial about his declining physique and there was no one on hand to guide him towards a more flattering image. Part of Elvis' appeal was always his homespun charm, but the fact that he was so deeply rooted in a provincial culture and his entourage of local boys, had left him without an honest companion or equal, who might have stepped in to image advise. As a result, the jumpsuits that had once showcased his athletic body – being made from stretched gabardine, a material favoured by ice skaters – became unforgiving and faintly absurd.

Elvis' white denim Tiger suit. Elvis was particularly fond of his costumes featuring tigers, as the motifs symbolised the ancient spiritual concepts embodied in martial arts, about which he was passionate.

Elvis wearing the Chinese Dragon Suit during a concert in Dayton in 1974.

Regrettably, this is the image that often springs to mind when one thinks of Elvis in the 1970s. But let us instead cast our minds back to the early 1970s, as the chisel-faced performer charismatically works the audiences in Las Vegas. His white jumpsuit is highlighted by the flashing strobe lights, making him appear as if in a series of frozen, animated frames. As James Burton plays a hot guitar solo, Elvis provides an equally incendiary air-guitar routine, and somehow, incredibly, looks super cool doing it! Elvis' command of the Las Vegas stage is remarkable, alternating dramatic karate moves, with crouching to cup the faces of adoring bouffant-haired fans in his hands and kiss them fully on the mouth. With ever-accelerating movements he builds towards the climax, the tension becoming almost unbearable, when suddenly, isolated by a single blue spotlight, he spins and drops to one knee, throwing his arms wide to embrace the blackened space before him as the final gold-encrusted curtain slowly descends.

The 1970s should be remembered as the period where Elvis truly pushed the fashion boundaries. As Presley's lifestyle reached levels of excess, so too did his fashion sense, as he embraced superhero capes, embellished jumpsuits and stage-wear as daywear.

Crowning Glory –
Elvis' Hair

Elvis sporting his famous pompadour hairstyle. The timeless style continues to influence contemporary performers, with Bruno Mars (who, incidentally started his show business career as an Elvis impersonator), Justin Timberlake, Rihanna and Gwen Stefani adopting variations of Elvis' rebel hairstyle.

While Presley borrowed his hair inspirations from others, he brought them together to create a style that was distinctively all-Elvis. Even as a high school student Elvis understood that hair was loaded with social meaning. While his fellow classmates sported the standard post-war short back and sides, Elvis set his sights higher and looked toward Hollywood's leading men for guidance. His references included the debonair Dean Martin, whose hair was worn indecently long for 1940s America, Marlon Brando's greaser style, and in particular Tony Curtis' pompadour, with which Elvis became enamoured after seeing him in *City Across the River* (1949). Presley lost no time in trying to coax his own hair into a greased, finger-curled coif, falling seductively across his forehead.

Curiously enough, Elvis' rockabilly pompadour had originally been conceived on the heads of aristocratic French women in the eighteenth century. The trend for wearing one's hair swept high off the forehead became popular after Madame de Pompadour, the influential mistress of Louis XV, sculpted her hair towards the heavens using a wire frame, straw padding and lashings of pomade. Noblewomen were soon adorning their fantastically high hairstyles with ribbons, feathers and even ornaments such as miniature wooden ships. The pomp continued to be worn predominantly by females, although an early tribe of English dandy known as the Macaroni took to wearing ridiculously tall pompadour wigs in the mid-eighteenth century. However, by the 1920s the androgynous pomp had started to also be worn more widely by men, assisted by the newly created hair pomades on the market.

When Elvis burst onto the scene, Hollywood had already witnessed on-screen bad boys such as James Dean and Marlon Brando sporting their own interpretations of the male pomp. However, Elvis' hair still managed to cause controversy, as it was higher, slicker and wilder than his contemporaries. His long, greased-back hair exhibited the same lack of conformity that would later be witnessed with punk Mohawks and skinhead No 1 cuts. Elvis' break-through quiff inspired a generation of teenage rebels globally, including the British Teddy Boys who used lashings of Brylcreem to imitate the slick, patent leather appearance of Elvis' style.

At the back of his head, Elvis wore a ducktail, also known as a duck's ass or D.A. for short. It was achieved by combing the hair from the ears to meet and overlap at the back of the head so it resembled the back of a duck. This style originated from the controversial 'Argentine ducktail', a long, slicked back hairstyle worn by young Latino American men in the 1940s. Outraged servicemen took to the streets of Los Angeles and attempted to publicly humiliate the immigrants by cutting the unorthodox hair from their heads. Shortly after, the ducktail entered the mainstream courtesy of a Philadelphia barber named Joe Cirello. His expertise at crafting the perfect seam down the back of the head made Cirello a hot ticket in the world of men's style. He was soon swept off to Hollywood to become the staff hairdresser at Warner Brothers Studio, where he would work on the hair of James Dean, Humphrey Bogart and, later in his career, Elvis – the man who had coincidentally also helped to bring the distinctive ducktail to the masses.

The young Elvis also threw into the mix a pair of menacing sideburns, adding a dose of rugged Southern truck driver to his look. The combination of the regal pompadour, the slick, provocative ducktail and the grassroots sideburns created a style that managed to be shockingly effeminate – further emphasised by Elvis' very public hair-combing performances – while at the same time also contentiously macho and working class.

Elvis would have been unable to achieve his early, gravity-defying hair-sculpture without the help of Royal Crown Hair Dressing pomade. The hair styling aid was created in 1936 and made on Elvis' doorstep in Memphis. During the 1950s and 60s, Royal Crown was marketed towards, and predominantly used by African-American consumers, as the rich oils offered long lasting moisture to afro-textured hair. While it is well documented that Elvis' music blurred racial boundaries in the 1950s American South, perhaps even the way he styled his hair and the products he chose could be seen as challenging these stringent parameters.

The performer Little Richard advertising Royal Crown Hair Dressing; Little Richard was known for his high, 'conk' hairstyle. This style was popular in the 1950s with young African American men, who used hot irons and hair-relaxing solutions, sculpting the front of the hair into a pompadour. The musician James Brown was also known for his high pomp around this time. Following the effects of the Black is Beautiful cultural movement of the 60s, a more natural, untreated Afro style became popular with both female and male African-Americans.

CLIENT: J. STRICKLAND & CO.
PUBLICATION: EBONY MAGAZINE
DEC. ½ PAGE, B&W—RCHR-MEN
AGENCY: NOBLE-DURY ADVERTISING
MEMPHIS • NASHVILLE

Elvis' early hairstyles owe much to this small tin of Royal Crown Hair Dressing. In the eighteenth century, hair pomades were unappealingly made from bear fat or lard, but by the time Elvis was sculpting his pomp, pomades mostly consisted of beeswax or were petroleum jelly based. Other popular styling aids from the era included Murray's Superior Pomade, Brylcreem and Dixie Peach Hair Pomade.

Elvis shaking his mane of rebellion, which conservative critics considered a threat to clean cut conformity in the 1950s. Elvis' wild, attention-grabbing hair, coupled with his provocative stage performances, challenged the values of keeping one's appearance, movements and sexuality under strict control.

Although Elvis' youthful hair screamed of disobedience, for much of his career it was actually being styled by his mother's hairdresser. Homer M. Gilleland, or 'Mr Gill' as his clients preferred, first met Gladys Presley while tending to her coiffure at a Memphis department store salon in the 1950s. As Elvis' fame grew, Mr Gill started to pay the whole Presley family home visits, initially at their Audubon Drive home, and then later at Graceland. Mr Gill coloured and trimmed Elvis' hair for over two decades. He was provided with his own credit card to travel across America at short notice for hairdressing commitments, including styling Elvis' hair for the 1973 *Aloha from Hawaii* satellite broadcast. Elvis repaid the hairdresser's dedication by presenting him with numerous gifts over the years, including a car and a family home in Memphis.

Elvis' hairstylist Mr Gill spent over two decades collecting hair clippings from the star's head as sacred mementos that documented the changing colours of Presley's hair. Celebrity hair has become a collectable commodity, with strands from the head of Che Guevara, John Lennon, Abraham Lincoln and Napoleon Bonaparte becoming particularly prized. However, Elvis still manages to top the list for the most expensive hair sold at auction, with a lock of his hair selling for $115,000 in 2002.

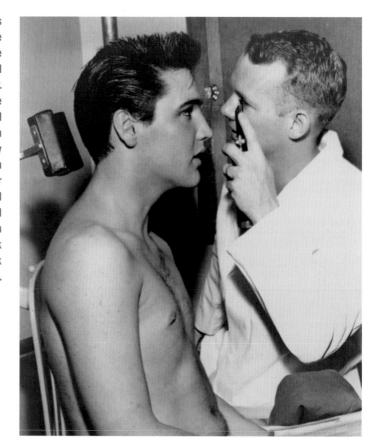

On 25th March 1958, Elvis received the most famous military haircut of the twentieth century when his trademark pompadour and sideburns were replaced with a standard GI cut. Having been inducted into the army, Elvis succumbed to barber's clippers while at Fort Chaffee, Arkansas. The world's media witnessed the Samson-like spectacle; with many heralding it as a symbolic moment in the demise of rock 'n' roll. Life magazine alone collected 1,200 photos from the session. 'Hair today, gone tomorrow' Elvis is said to have quipped in good humour, although he later spoke of the distress that he was covering up. The haircut also grieved his fans, causing some to shed tears at the sight of Elvis' fallen locks. The scene was later dramatised in the feature film *Bye-Bye Birdie*, starring Ann-Margret.

Following his release from the army Elvis was unable to reclaim control of his hair, with his Hollywood film roles now largely dictating his styles. Although he sported a rugged beard in *Charro!,* a loose fringe in *Clambake* and an impressive pair of mutton chops in *The Trouble with Girls*, in general his overall appearance was clean-shaven and disciplined during the 1960s. Whilst performers such as the Beatles, Jim Morrison and Jimi Hendrix flaunted their individual freedom by growing their hair long, in comparison Elvis' coiffure could often appear somewhat artificial and contrived. Producer Hal Wallis was so concerned with the wig-like appearance of Elvis' hair in *Viva Las Vegas* that he took it upon himself to write to Presley's management, alerting them to the detrimental effect that moulded-looking hair could have on Elvis' long-term career.

Madonna's Hollywood hairdresser, Andy Lecompte, believes that Elvis' addiction to hair dye was responsible for the rigid style. 'Elvis naturally had lush brown hair, but it was in the 1960s that he became obsessed with dyeing his hair the darkest shade of blue black'. Having previously used pomade to make his sandy hair appear darker, in the late 1950s Elvis had started to sporadically dye his hair black to create a more dramatic onscreen presence. By the 1960s, Elvis was having a full dye-job every fortnight; with daily root touch-ups while on set to ensure continuity. Presley's hairdressers would use home dye kits, such as Clairol *Black Velvet* or L'Oreal *Excellence Blue Black* to create the dark, patent leather effect. 'When the hair becomes that solid in colour it lacks dimension and is unable to catch the light in any way. This resulted in Elvis' hair during the era often appearing quite solid and lacking in movement' Lecompte observes.

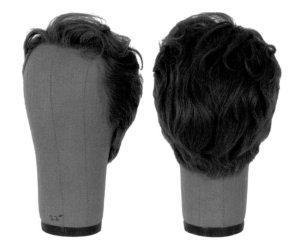

Elvis' blonde wig from the MGM film *Kissin' Cousins* (1964). Elvis played the dual roles of two look-alike cousins, differentiated by their hair colour. The British hairstylist Sydney Guilaroff, who had also worked on *North by Northwest* and *The Graduate* was responsible for the hair.

It was in the mid-60s that Elvis met a young hair stylist who had a profound effect not only on his appearance, but also his personal development. Larry Geller was an LA hairdresser whose client list included Marlon Brando and Steve McQueen. Geller had been recommended by Elvis' Hollywood hairdresser, Sal Orifice, and was invited to the star's Perugia Way house to style the star's raven locks. The instant rapport between the pair led to Geller being employed as Elvis' full time hairstylist and spiritual adviser, recommending mind-expanding books for the star to read. Hair loss was a big concern for Elvis, who told Geller that the main priority was to keep his hair on his head. Geller turned to health food stores to source vitamin capsules and Aloe Vera, mixing them with a base shampoo and herbs to create a bespoke hair wash for his client. Vitamin E, liquid Biotin and Jojoba oil were combined to create a nourishing conditioning treatment to keep Elvis' hair baby soft and rectify the damage from the hair dyes. Aside from a five-year gap – when Geller was discharged due to Elvis' inner circle questioning the influence he held over the star – Geller worked on Elvis' hair for the rest of his lifetime, finally styling Presley's hair for his funeral.

By the 1970s, Elvis hair was becoming as extreme as his stage costumes.

His youthful sideburns had now morphed into a bushy pair of mutton chops, a style of facial hair grown at the side of the face to extend the hairline to below the ears and along the jaw. Mutton chops had become popular during the American Civil War, but by the time Elvis was wearing them in the 1970s, he was in good company as stars including John Lennon, Clint Eastwood and Sean Connery were also framing their faces with impressive side-whiskers.

Elvis' hair was grown long and allowed to move freely on stage, falling across his face before being theatrically swept back into place, in a gesture reminiscent of his 1950s stage act. Elvis memorably revived his famous pompadour for the *Aloha from Hawaii* concert but this time it was updated with textured layers framing the face, set with waves of hairspray. 'Elvis' longer hair during the Vegas years is pure 1970s' observes the British celebrity hairdresser Trevor Sorbie. 'The trend was for overgrown but styled hair, which embraced a hippy sensibility with the sideburns, but was still well coiffed and quite bouffant. This then morphed into shaggy styles and even mullets, so is a look many people are happy to leave in the past!' While Elvis had never been one for effortless hair, in the final years of his life it became particularly high maintenance as his prematurely white hair needed constant retouching, with his eyebrows and lashes also dyed to coordinate.

Although Elvis experimented with many hairstyles during his lifetime, it is his high-gloss pompadour that still continues to top the best hairstyle lists. 'Elvis' 1950s quiff is still influencing male hair trends today. It's one of the most popular styles you see on younger men and is especially popular with footballers and "metrosexuals". It's artfully dishevelled – so has been styled and set, but maintains a low-key nonchalance' Sorbie concludes. Elvis' pomp is able to continually reinvent itself, offering each generation a template for how to style their hair with attitude.

Contemporary Japanese rockabillies have taken Elvis' pomp to new heights, parading their towering bouffants around Tokyo's Yoyogi Park.

The counter at
the The Arcade
Restaurant in
Memphis, which
was a favourite of
Elvis' in the 1950s.

'I like it well done. I ain't orderin' a pet.'
Elvis Presley, stating how he liked his meat cooked.

THREE

Elvis Food

It is early evening at Graceland and the kitchen suddenly springs into life as the nocturnal master of the house finally wakes, ready for his breakfast. The team of cooks; Pauline, Mary, Alberta, Lottie and Nancy, work in shifts to provide catering 24 hours of the day. They begin preparing Elvis' standard breakfast of a pound of burnt bacon, sausages, five scrambled eggs and biscuits dipped in butter. While The King has slumbered, the women have also whipped up a selection of desserts, including favourites such as banana pudding, brownies, apple pie and sweet potato pie.

If Elvis' entourage is at Graceland, the kitchen is a frenzy of activity, responding to the endless food requests. Mary Jenkins, Elvis' cook for 14 years, estimated that when there was a full house, the Graceland food bills could be anywhere between $300 and $400 per day. On a quiet day Elvis is happy to eat his meals on a tray on his lap, often in bed, or in the Jungle Room watching TV.

Elvis grew fond of pineapples during his time spent in Hawaii while filming or on vacation. When he returned back to Graceland, he would ask his cooks to give him a slice of Hawaii with a pineapple upside-down cake.

It had not always been so. Growing up in the poverty of Tupelo during The Great Depression, Elvis' early diet had been extremely basic and consisted primarily of grits, bread and lard, with meat being a weekly treat. Vegetables, including okra, eggplant, tomatoes and collard greens were provided courtesy of Aunt Lillian's 'truck patch' in her backyard. Times were hard, although contrary to popular belief, it is unlikely that Elvis resorted to eating squirrel as a child. Dr Ted M. Ownby, Director of the Center for the Study of Southern Culture at the University of Mississippi, observes that 'Elvis' parents came from farm people and were part of an important late industrial change that came to north-eastern Mississippi. The region became a popular place for relatively low-wage industries – the kinds that wanted young white women to sew or young white men to work in furniture factories. His mother Gladys, as a teenager, had worked in both the fields in Pontotoc County and at least one garment factory in Lee County before marrying Vernon Presley. From all we know, Vernon Presley did all sorts of jobs but, as the song says, "never picked cotton".'

Dr Ownby makes an important distinction between Elvis' upbringing and the experience of growing up in a poor, traditional farming household. 'Elvis' parents were trying to make ends meet outside an agricultural economy that no longer worked for people of their incomes. So, Elvis grew up seeing his parents worrying about debt and bills, but he did not grow up working in the fields or contributing to the household through hunting and fishing. Therefore it seems unlikely that Elvis ate squirrel and other last-refuge meals of rural people, though it seems highly possible that his parents had as children' Dr Ownby observes. The Presley's meagre lifestyle took a turn for the worse when Elvis' father was sent to prison for allegedly forging a cheque. Elvis' diet became even more restricted and he would sometimes have to survive on grits and cheese for weeks on end. Money was still tight when Elvis became a high school student and he was frequently unable to afford the canteen lunches.

Johnnies Drive In, Tupelo, Mississippi. Although Elvis rarely had the funds to eat out while growing up, he would occasionally stop by at Johnnies for a cheeseburger and RC Cola, while attending nearby Lawhon Elementary School.

These early food experiences greatly shaped Elvis' adult diet, and in many ways his palate never really matured past the idiosyncratic tastes of a child or adolescent. He ate as if let loose at the buffet table of a kid's birthday party, snacking on popsicles, donuts, milkshakes, Pepsi Cola and cheeseburgers throughout the day. Having found fame and fortune, Elvis would hire out the local Memphis cinemas or fairground and indulge in an unlimited supply of candyfloss, hot dogs and popcorn. Like an infant, Elvis would also ask for his meal to be cut into bite-sized chunks before it was served to him and he preferred to be fed on demand rather than follow a strict schedule.

While his fellow celebrities were entertaining the paparazzi in ultra-exclusive Hollywood restaurants such as Dominick's or La Dolce Vita, Elvis shunned this scene and ate either in his hotel suite or at home. Even his choice of home cooking set him apart from his contemporaries. While the Kennedys had installed a French gourmet chef at the White House, and Frank Sinatra had an Italian personal chef, Elvis employed local women who cooked simple cuisine, in the style of his mother's Southern cooking. Dinner-time favourites at Graceland, usually eaten at about 1:00am, included black-eyed peas, fried okra, creamed potatoes, crowder peas, meatloaf, corn bread, chicken fried steak, burgers, pork chops with sauerkraut (a nod to his time in Germany) and porterhouse steaks, cooked to an ash. 'I like it well done. I ain't orderin' a pet', Elvis would state.

The Presley family favourite, meatloaf. Also known as the 'Vitality Loaf', the dish has historically gained popularity when times are hard. When Elvis was an infant during The Great Depression, meatloaf offered the family a frugal way to combine cheap meat and leftovers. Elvis continued to enjoy the dish as a comfort food throughout his adult life.

The Rendezvous ribs, which Elvis would enjoy within the comfort of his own home.

If take-out food were on the menu, Elvis would occasionally sample the local Memphis specialty of barbecue pork. Ribs would be ordered from the famous Rendezvous restaurant in Downtown Memphis. John Vergos, the founder's son explains that 'Elvis loved our ribs. However, he never came to The Rendezvous. Elvis always wanted to rent the whole place out and my father didn't want to lose customers so he refused. Instead, we would courier our ribs out to Graceland for Elvis to enjoy'. Elvis was not alone in his desire to eat a pre-prepared meal in the comfort of his own home. From the 1950s onwards the take-out meal boomed in popularity, with drive-throughs and franchised fast food chains springing up throughout America. The take-out meal, which can be historically traced back to the Ancient Roman times, fitted easily into Elvis' schedule, which had continued to be erratic since he had started touring at the onset of his career. As Elvis' fame increased and he risked being mobbed by fans in public, the take-out seemed the safest option – although it also added to Elvis' impending isolation from the outside world.

In Elvis' world, however, there were a few meals that warranted a personal appearance. In 1976, Elvis famously flew in his personal plane from Memphis to Denver just to sample the Fool's Gold Loaf. The sandwich was conceived in Denver, at a high-end steak house called the Colorado Mine Company. Working in their kitchen was a 16-year-old chef named Nick Andurlakis, who was searching for a way to invigorate the menu. 'We all put our heads together and came up with the peanut butter, jelly and bacon sandwich. It was a gag-item really – we wanted something fun on the menu, just for laughs' Andurlakis remembers. The 4-pound sandwich consists of a 1-pound sourdough loaf, cut lengthwise three times. Next, 1-pound of peanut butter and 1-pound of Dickinson's blueberry preserves are added, topped off with a pound of crispy bacon. The dish is served in a mining pan and packs in an estimated 8,000 calories.

Andurlakis says that during their acquaintance, he saw nothing remarkable in Elvis' appetite. 'Everyone thinks Elvis was this big eater, but when he was in The Mine Company, he truly was just an average eater. He certainly didn't scoff down everything he touched' he adds. The last time Andurlakis saw Elvis they discussed the possibility of opening a restaurant together in Memphis. 'Elvis gave me a big hug and said "I'll be back"' recalls Andurlakis, who now has his own Colorado restaurant called 'Nick's Café: Home of the Fool's Gold Loaf'. The walls are lined with rare Elvis photos and memorabilia, and he has even kept the mining tin that he once served Elvis his sandwich in. Andurlakis feels that Elvis shunned the bright lights of the celebrity restaurant scene because he preferred the freedom and privacy that a local, anonymous eatery could offer. 'In his heart, Elvis was always a boy from back home. When he visited us, he just ran around and did what he wanted to do, without anyone watching him' Andurlakis observes.

COLORADO MINE
specialties

~❦~

---

drink at your own risk!

"JOSE' FLOORBANGER"
Tequila, Galliano and a squeeze of Lime

"DUST CUTTER"
Light Rum, Grapefruit and Pineapple Juice

"THE SLICK MENDOZA MEMORIAL COCKTAIL"
Vodka, Bouillon and Lime

"NORWEGIAN VACATION"
Aquavit and Beer

"BLASTING POWDER"
190 proof Silk Hat Grain,
110 proof Green Chartreuse
and White Creme de Cocoa

"COMING & GOING"
Metaxa, Brandy and Prune Juice

"THE MIND SHAFT"
190 proof Silk Hat Grain and Blue Curacao

"THE ZAMBOANGA HUMMER"
From the South Pacific,
exotic ingredients too
numerous to mention

**"THE KANDY COLORED,
TANGERINE FLAKE,
STREAMLINED BABY"**
Apricot Brandy, Vodka, Cream,
Tangerine Juice, laced
with Creme de Almond

THE COLORADO MINE COMPANY

serves exclusively:

CHIVAS REGAL
12 year old Scotch

WILD TURKEY
101 proof Straight Kentucky Bourbon

SEAGRAMS CROWN ROYAL
Blended Canadian Whisky

BOODLES
British Gin

STOLICHNAYA
imported Russian Vodka

~❦~

THE BEEF
Exclusively From
CENTRAL PACKING CO. OF COLORADO
Only the Finest Beef is Hand Selected
and Aged by Our Chefs

❦ DINNER ❦
Served with SUPERB salad
. . . a blending of select greens including Boston head lettuce and romaine with choice of dressings
and HOT MINERS SOURDOUGH BISCUITS
Piping Hot, Guaranteed Fresh-Baked Every Day In Our Own Ovens

MINERS SPECIAL
A large thick cut of Colorado Prime Rib with au jus
SECOND HELPINGS, OUR PLEASURE
. . . NO CHARGE
11.95

PRIME RIB or STEAK and LOBSTER
A generous cut of Prime Rib or a choice cut of Top
Sirloin and a select Australian Lobster Tail
17.95

24 OZ. T-BONE STEAK 12.95
The old miners' favorite steak

ALASKAN KING CRAB LEGS 13.95
Steamed and served with drawn butter

NEW YORK STRIP STEAK 11.95
A juicy, 16oz. cut, seared and flame broiled

RAINBOW TROUT 10.95
Fresh from the cool mountain streams of Colorado
Pan fried and served boned with lemon and tartar sauce

TOP SIRLOIN STEAK 10.95
An extra thick, special cut, of Prime Tender Beef

LOBSTER TAIL 17.95
An extra large select Australian lobster tail
butter brushed and boiled

GROUND SIRLOIN 5.95
A full pound of Prime ground sirloin, broiled to perfection.
Topped with Roquefort, Pancho sauce or smothered with onions

DOVER SOLE 12.95
Boned, grilled, and served with choice of Tartar,
Remoulade, Pancho, or Amandine sauce . . . on the side

BEEF KABOB TERIYAKI 10.95
Tender beef chunks served with onion, tomato,
green pepper and mushrooms on a bed of rice

BUTTERFLY SHRIMP 11.95
Jumbo shrimp, butterflied, lightly breaded and deep fried

PEPPER STEAK 11.95
Juicy New York cut seasoned with fresh cracked pepper

FOOLS GOLD 37.95
A peanut butter and jelly sandwich with an exceptional flair—
rare combination of creamery peanut butter and blueberry ja
served on a sourdough loaf with crisp bacon
This price is negotiable. (Inflation is killin' us!)

PRIME FILET MIGNON 12.95
A thick cut with a mushroom cap.
Wrapped in bacon if you wish or topped with Bernaise Sauce

LAMB A PLATEFUL **PORK**
tender baby chops split & served thin or Greek style **12.95** | stuffed double chops **10.95**

PROBABLY THE WORLD'S GREATEST FRIED CHICKEN
Prepared in a rich southern batter
and served with sourdough biscuits and gravy
7.95

KEITH BROWN'S FAVORITE SANDWICH 6.95
New York Steak or Prime Rib
❦❦❦
GIANT Baked Potato - butter or sour cream 1.25 Sauteed Mushrooms - a skillet full 3.00
Stuffed Baked Potato 1.50 French Fried Onion Rings 1.75 Broccoli 1.50
Deep Fried Zucchini - a heaping pan full - enough for your table 2.50
Vegetable Platter - freshly steamed vegetable assortment 2.75
Miners Fried Spuds Our Specialty - A Lot Of Them For 2.00

DESSERTS 1.75
French Vanilla Ice Cream served with your choice of Liqueur toppings
Old Fashioned Hot Fudge Sundae topped with whipped cream and a cherry

BEVERAGES .75
We are affiliated with BankAmericard, American Express and Master Charge   We accept checks only with a guarantee check car

---

The original menu from The Colorado Mine Company, home of the famous Fool's Gold Loaf sandwich, which was on the menu for $37.95.

The Arcade Diner in Memphis is famed for its fried peanut butter and banana sandwich, which you can eat in the same booth that Elvis favoured. Although Elvis was a frequent visitor to the restaurant in the 1950s, he actually opted for the more traditional, Southern style dishes that they served at that time.

Although the Fool's Gold Loaf may seem like a superstar's extravagance, it is really just an elevated version of the peanut butter and banana sandwich that Elvis' mother had fed him when he was growing up. Gladys would fry the white bread in fat and add bacon if it was available. For a child, this sandwich must also have seemed an indulgent treat, but as Dr Ted M. Ownby from the University of Mississippi explains, it also has an interesting cultural origin. 'Elvis' famed favourite meal of peanut butter and banana sandwich is intriguing to consider as part of a twentieth-century South. Bananas were a sweet treat from South America. Elvis could have chosen molasses or sweet potato pie, but he chose something exotic – a small luxury available for purchase. Peanut butter was a new thing, famously developed in the South but likely not part of his parents' or certainly his grandparents' diet – the Peter Pan and Skippy brands started in the 1920s and 30s. And sandwiches themselves were the products of mobility, not standard parts of farm meals'.

The peanut butter and banana sandwich continues to hold its place in popular culture. 'Let's not mess around: you want trashy, I'll give you trashy – I'll give you The King' said the celebrity chef Nigella Lawson when introducing her attenuated version of the recipe. The Arcade Restaurant in Memphis continues to be the Elvis sandwich temple, as fans from across the globe flock to sample their fried peanut butter and banana sandwich in the original booth where Elvis once sat. The Arcade has the honour of being Memphis' oldest restaurant, having opened in 1919. Elvis was a regular visitor in the 1950s, often accompanied by the Memphis disc jockey Dewey Phillips. The duo would sit at the booth at the back of the restaurant, conveniently located next to the back door in case Elvis needed to make a dash from his enthusiastic fans. Harry Zepatos, the third-generation owner of the Arcade, says that although the peanut butter and banana sandwich is one of the most popular items on the menu, when Elvis visited he would actually 'come in for traditional Southern cooking – meat and vegetables. He also liked the black-eyed peas and mashed potatoes'.

Although Elvis' weight fluctuated throughout his lifetime, for a man consuming such a calorific diet, he managed to stay in relatively good shape for the majority of the time. This battle against the bulge was achieved through a combination of diet pills (first taken when Elvis was drafted into the army) and intensive bouts of exercise. His particular passions were karate, which he practised for two decades, and racquetball, which he played frequently at his court in Graceland.

In the final few years, however, Elvis' health had started to deteriorate and his weight ballooned. A diet list was mounted on the wall of Graceland's kitchen, which went largely ignored. Nancy Rooks, a long-term Graceland cook, said that if she ever tried to moderate Elvis' food intake by taking food off his plate, he would watch her on the in-house CCTV and 'he'd be upset. I'd have to come back downstairs and put it back on his plate'. During prolonged hospital visits, both his staff and the nurses would smuggle comfort food in for him.

The façade and interior of the Arcade Restaurant in Memphis. The nostalgic 1950s décor has been used for scenes in films including *Walk the Line, The Firm, Great Balls of Fire* and *Mystery Train*.

The Elvis Booth at the Arcade Restaurant in Memphis.

In 1976 Elvis made his sole business investment venture, *Presley's Center Courts Racquetball Club* in Memphis. Land was purchased, construction and plans were organised, bank accounts were opened, and business cards and merchandising (as pictured) were created. The venture had cost over a million dollars before it had even opened and Elvis soon became panicked at the spiralling costs. Elvis and his partner Linda Thompson attended the opening of the centre in April 1976 but the project was wound down and closed within a few months.

Unable, or unwilling to commit to a healthier lifestyle, Elvis considered an intestinal bypass, but shelved the idea when the doctor stressed that he would still have to control his diet post-operation. Instead, fad diets were used, including the yoghurt diet and a diet that consisted solely of Jell-O, both failing to produce lasting results. In desperation, in 1974 Elvis attempted his most extreme fast – The Sleep Diet. Las Vegas-based Dr Elias Ghanem advocated the diet that used sedatives to induce sleep, while consuming a predominantly liquid diet. The programme was cut short after a drowsy Elvis fell from his bed and concluded that there must be an easier way to shed the pounds.

Perhaps due to the sheer quantity of food he consumed, one often associates Elvis' diet with unbridled extravagance. However, one of the most surprising aspects of Elvis' dining is actually how simple and modest his tastes were. Elvis made a conscious decision not to dine in the finest restaurants, or hire world-renowned chefs to cook at Graceland. In fact, the young Priscilla put a stop to Elvis' entourage ordering prime steaks from the kitchen at home – it was seen as excessive as Elvis himself usually just ordered hamburgers or peanut butter and banana sandwiches. Elvis' diet, as with so many other aspects of his life, remained faithful to his provincial culture and went against the grain of how a megastar is expected to behave. Perhaps it is just another indication of how little Elvis' wealth and elevated status actually meant to him. At the end of the day, what else is there for a lonesome down-home boy to spend his millions on but hamburgers and the faint remembrance of his mother's cooking?

Elvis trained in karate from 1970–74 under Master Kang Rhee in Memphis and would often incorporate the moves he learnt into his stage routine. Within the training area Elvis was referred to as Mr Tiger. Always keen to stand out from the crowd, Elvis asked Master Kang Rhee to design this special uniform for him to wear for a karate demonstration. On his left chest is a badge showing Elvis' TCB logo, while the left sleeve has a badge showing a fist, with a crown above it. Yong Rhee (son of Master Kang Rhee) says that the bespoke uniform was designed because 'Elvis had his own distinct style. He was very passionate about martial arts training and he wanted his uniform to reflect his personality'.

FOUR

'You know, when some people get down and out, they go out and get drunk and forget it all. Me, I just go out and buy another car'

Elvis Presley.

Elvis-Mobiles

Elvis and shiny new Cadillacs – it was an irresistible combination. Elvis adored Cadillacs. He sang about them, customised and collected them, and gave them to others as if they were candy bars. Both Elvis and the iconic car came to represent an era when the world's most powerful nation was at its most confident. Throughout the 1950s, Elvis' rising fame coincided with the boom in American car production, with the US making two-thirds of the vehicles in the world. An entire industry of drive-throughs swiftly sprang up, offering cinemas, diners, banks and even church services, all from the comfort of your car. Cheap gas, fewer cars on the road and a plethora of spacious, luxurious models to choose made the 1950s a golden era for the driver. Influential car designers such as Harley Earl of General Motors (Cadillac's parent company) embarked on flights of fancy, creating fantastical automobiles that imitated rockets and fighter planes, clad in glistening chrome and sprouting oversized tail fins that grew ever larger as the decade progressed.

The Cadillac became Elvis' status symbol and a barometer of how far he had come from the hardship of his childhood. 'When I was a kid I'd sit on our porch and watch those long, low cars whizz by. I told myself then that when I was grown, I was gonna have me, not one, but two Cadillacs sitting out front of Mama's and Daddy's. Well Sir, I guess you can say I've done a little better than that' he proudly told reporters.

Detail of a classic Cadillac car, Elvis' favourite style of automobile.

Elvis was not alone in his desire to acquire a Cadillac and all the associations that came with it. In their book *Driving Passion*, Marsh and Collett state that owning a Cadillac has long represented the pinnacle of social achievement, 'a visible sign that one has arrived in more sense than one'. However, post-war it joined the ranks of production-line cars and the symbolism changed. 'Cadillacs now became the costume of the *nouveau riche*…people who are busy clambering up the social ladder still imagine that those at the top share their reverence for Cadillacs. They are wrong. The last thing that someone who has always had money wants to do is adopt the style of someone who has only just acquired it'. Unconcerned with these silent class-war allegiances, Elvis fulfilled his childhood fantasy by turning his driveway into a merry-go-round of interchangeable Cadillacs, which were continuously upgraded or repainted in a celebration of two-tone colour combinations.

'Elvis loved Cadillacs primarily because they were made in the USA' says George Barris, the Hollywood car customiser who created many of Elvis' bespoke autos. Barris is famed for constructing the Batmobile, and his personal client list also included Elvis' idols, James Dean and Liberace. 'I worked on around a dozen autos for Elvis – a number for his films and some for his personal use. The design, comfort and luxury of the Cadillac gave Elvis a lot of enjoyment. He didn't really go for fancy European cars'.

The renowned behavioural psychologist Dr Peter Collett comments that 'it was no wonder that Elvis aligned himself with the Cadillac. These cars are all to do with theatre – they are really designed for the people standing on the side of the street.' Collett draws a parallel between 'the essential disutility and pure spectacle of Elvis' stage-wear and the kind of cars he drove. The tassels on Elvis' jumpsuit remind me of the wings on a Cadillac. They were both there to create an illusion. It is all to do with spectacle and theatre'.

Although Elvis had a love affair with the Cadillac that lasted more than two decades, he also had dalliances with other makes and models of cars throughout his lifetime. In 1970, Elvis went head-to-head with Frank Sinatra to buy the only Stutz Blackhawk prototype available for sale on the market at that time. Having agreed to pose for publicity photos with the car (a requirement that Sinatra flatly refused) Elvis was soon the satisfied owner of the treasured car from the recently revived Stutz Motor Company, who were famed for creating America's first sports car in 1911. Elvis enjoyed the car so much that he developed a fleeting infatuation with the Stutz Blackhawk, buying three models in consecutive years.

This is the second Stutz Blackhawk car that Elvis owned. The two-seater car was delivered to his Beverly Hills home in 1971 and featured the most cutting-edge audio system that money could buy.

**One of Elvis'
Harley-Davidson
motorcycles.**

However, the garage at Graceland wasn't just brimming with luxurious cars. Elvis also had a prized collection of motorbikes and loved to race around Memphis at night, more often than not with an attractive girl perched on the back of the bike. His motorcycle fleet included a vintage Honda Dream, Harley-Davidson Panhead and a Triumph, but his favoured bike was the Harley-Davidson Dresser – a monstrous touring bike in the style of a police bike, with a large windshield and upright seat. In homage to his rural roots, Elvis also kept an old John Deere tractor at home and would hook it up to a wagon for boisterous rides around the grounds.

In many ways, Elvis' car buying obsession was a form of showmanship, which attempted to extend his stage presence into the civic world. As the local media arrived to report on Elvis' latest shopping spree, interviewing the bewildered salesperson, Elvis' car purchasing became a mode of public theatre. Fantasy also played a strong role in the interior design of Elvis' cars. George Barris recalls that 'Elvis requested that round portholes be put into a Cadillac so he could feel as if he was driving a yacht, and that surfboards be used for seats in a hot rod roadster, as Elvis liked the feeling that he was just about to hit the waves while driving'. Elvis appreciated George Barris' customisation skills so much that he even commissioned him to decorate his Hollywood home with car parts. 'Decorating the house was an interesting thing to do but I could never really keep up with what he liked and what he didn't like' recalls Barris.

Dr Peter Collett says that this type of car customisation could be compared to buying a bespoke suit, tailored to your personal requirements. 'However, I think it was about more than just the spectacle. The type of customisation Elvis had commissioned was created for conversations with other people. In other words, it gave him things to talk about with his mates – it was something to be reflected on and enjoyed with others. It was also a way of distinguishing oneself, of being creative and imposing something of yourself on the medium' he says.

Here is a look at some of highlights of Elvis' lifelong passion for automobiles – from the beat-up Tupelo get-away car, to his most extravagant gold-plated Cadillac.

The car that helped to change history. This is a replica of the 1939 green Plymouth Sedan used to transport the Presley family to Memphis in 1948. 'We were broke, man, broke. We left Tupelo overnight. Dad packed all our belongings in boxes and put them in the trunk and on top of a 1939 Plymouth. We just headed for Memphis. Things had to be better' Elvis later recalled.

The Hollywood dream machine. Elvis and his Continental Mark II. The car had been designed to recapture the spirit of a pre-war classic car, but the hefty production costs made it a short-lived fad.

The Continental Mark II was one of the most expensive autos on the road when it launched in 1955, with a price tag that matched the Rolls-Royce. Although this made it far beyond the realm of the average consumer, the idea behind the Continental Mark II was to create a buzz of interest and upstage other luxury autos such as the Packard or Cadillac. Stories of potential customers being turned away as they didn't have the right image and of Elizabeth Taylor having hers painted to match her eye colour, added to the car's aura of exclusivity. Apparently the car was so precious that it left the factory in its own flannel-lined bag, which could only be opened when it reached the dealer. It may have been a headline-grabber, but the car made dreadful business sense. The meticulous finishes and man-power needed to hand-assemble the Continental Mark II, meant that Ford Motor Company actually lost money on each of the 3,000 models that they eventually sold. Unsurprisingly, it was soon phased out.

Elvis bought this car in Miami in 1956. He had been driving around town in one of his trusty Cadillacs, but when the fans discovered it was his car they had covered it in declarations of love and telephone numbers. Elvis decided it was time for a change and paid the full $10,000 asking price for the Continental Mark II. It was a typical example of the spontaneity that Elvis used when buying his cars. 'He was very nonchalant about his motorcar collection. It was all done in a very relaxed, unique way' says George Barris.

The elegant design of the Continental Mark II referenced the early Ford Thunderbird model. Very little chrome was used in comparison to other cars of the 1950s.

Elvis on four wheels – the gold Cadillac that became Presley's stand-in.

In 1968 Elvis was preoccupied with resurrecting his music career, so his record company came up with the bizarre decision that an Eldorado Brougham Cadillac could stand in and tour across Australia in the performer's absence. This was not the first time that Elvis had been substituted by a car – in 1955 Elvis gave his mother a Cadillac Fleetwood Series 60, painted in his trademark colours of pink and black. Gladys Presley couldn't drive it as she didn't hold a licence, yet it became her pride and joy, acting as a visual reminder of her beloved absent son while he was on tour.

Elvis' 1960 Series 75 Fleetwood Limousine toured Australia for nine months, allowing it to be seen by 400,000 enthusiastic fans. Each visited town or city would elect an attractive young woman as their chosen 'Golden Girl' with the responsibility of safeguarding Elvis' luxury car. Before the car left for Australia, Elvis had organised for it to be filled with $1,000 worth of toys to be given to disadvantaged children and all profits from the tour were given to the Benevolent Society of New South Wales.

The Elvis substitute. Elvis posing with the gold Cadillac before it departs for its international tour. The entertainment console and white fur carpets can be seen in the lower photos.

Aside from the fact that the car had been touched by greatness, the limo's main draw was that it had been extravagantly pimped-up by the 'King of Kustomizers' George Barris. It was a big operation, even by Barris' standards. 'I had twenty men working on the limo in my shop. When Elvis visited us, he would meet and greet each person, having his photo taken with them. He was a gentleman, always polite and nice to everyone around him' Barris recalls. At a cost of $65,000 (the equivalent to almost half a million dollars now) the car was painted with 40 coats of crushed diamonds, mixed with Oriental fish scales. Portholes were added to the back windows, and the door handles, hubcaps and wing mirrors were plated in 24-carat gold. Once inside the car, Elvis could recline on a French-pearl-studded seat, kick his shoes off and rub his feet into the plush, white fur carpet, while watching his gold-plated colour television set. There was even a cocktail bar, a fur-lined vanity dresser and a gold telephone for Elvis' personal use. The outside world could be kept at bay by closing the monogrammed E.P. gold lamé curtains. It was pure decadence, on four wheels. When the car returned to America, it was the guest of honour at a banquet for 250 dignitaries in Atlanta. As the distinguished guests sat down to eat, overlooked by the gold Caddy, it may have occurred to them that they were experiencing the ultimate in symbolic representation – in the hearts and minds of the people, the car had quite literally been transformed into The King on Wheels.

For an exhibitionist like Elvis, the customised 1973 Grand Ville would have been the ultimate ride. It featured a vast set of horns mounted onto the front of the bonnet and silver guns for door handles. Images of totem poles, Native American chiefs in traditional headdress, wagons and cactuses were used to decorate the tooled leather seats. No inch of interior was left bare, with dollar coins sprinkled across the dashboard and inside doors, and there was even a miniature saddle secured to the back seat for young rodeo riders.

The swashbuckling tailor Nudie Cohn had created this theatrical beauty for Elvis, but regrettably was denied the opportunity to gift it to the star. It soon caught the eye of the country music singer Buck Owens, as Jim Shaw from Buck Owens Production Co, explains. 'Buck would travel to Nudie's Hollywood store on a regular basis to have his and the band's (the Buckaroos) suits made, and on a few consecutive trips saw this customised Pontiac Grand Ville sitting in the back of the shop'. Eventually Buck asked Nudie to tell him more about the personalised car. 'Nudie told Buck that he had gotten an opportunity to meet Elvis, and sold him a hundred thousand dollars' worth of suits! He wanted to sell him more, but Presley's people were keeping him away from Elvis to prevent any more of these "outrageous" sales. Nudie decided he was going to build one of his customised cars and present it to Elvis as a gift, thereby putting himself in the position to sell him a lot more suits!'

'Unfortunately, Elvis's handlers wouldn't even let him near Elvis to give him the car, and Nudie was frustrated and angry. He told Buck he was ready to sell the car to the first person who would give him what he had invested in it. Buck asked him how much that was and Nudie told him $11,000. Buck said, "I'll take it!"' Shaw recounts. Elvis' management may well have been fearful of yet another spending spree, or perhaps the flamboyant car was considered just too outrageous, even for Elvis' image.

The custom-cruiser now hangs above the bar at Buck Owens's Crystal Palace, an entertainment complex in California. 'I don't know if Elvis even wanted the car – it could have been a publicity thing' says Nudie Cohn's granddaughter, Jamie Nudie. 'My grandfather made eighteen cars throughout his career, which were called the Nudie Mobiles' she says of the attention-grabbing motors, which are now considered highly collectable.

The almost-Elvis Nudie Mobile. The sensational car now hangs above the bar at Buck Owens's Crystal Palace.

Detail of the highly decorative seats and miniature leather saddle, covered in silver dollars.

The white 1973 Cadillac Eldorado Custom Coupe, which Elvis bought from Madison Cadillac for $10,000. Apparently the car was gifted to the karate instructor Master Kang Rhee, under whom Elvis trained from 1970–74. The car now resides at the National Automobile Museum in Reno, alongside cars once owned by James Dean and John F. Kennedy.

Wanting to transport his instruments and luggage around in style, but with Cadillac yet to bring out a station wagon, Elvis took matters into his own hands and had this 1974 Deville station wagon custom-made by Madison Cadillac, at a cost of just over $17,000. This do-it-yourself attitude often resulted in cars that looked good in photos, but less than immaculate when viewed close up. Dr Peter Collett notes that this is often a factor of American cars and particularly the type of autos that Elvis favoured. 'These cars, whether they were for the movies or for Elvis' consumption, were really designed to be seen as visual images. They didn't have to be properly finished off or in top condition to make an impression' he says.

This wagon was sold to a private collector and went under the radar for 37 years, before being purchased by Volo Auto Museum and displayed as part of their collection, along with the legal documentation and a photograph of the car outside Graceland. 'We were the first people to ever display the car. Many of the Elvis historians didn't even know the car existed until we brought it into the limelight' says Brian Grams from the Volo Auto Museum.

The Presley hybrid. Elvis' DIY attitude extended to his automobiles, as seen with this Cadillac wagon that was made especially for the star. The car can be seen on the driveway of Graceland in this photo.

Elvis bought this 1971 De Tomaso Pantera on the used car market for $2,400 in 1974, as a gift for his girlfriend Linda Thompson. Elvis had a fit of rage when the sports car wouldn't start and pulled out his handgun, shooting it repeatedly. The car still retains the bullet holes, visible in the top image. This model was the result of the collaboration between the Ford Motor Company and the Italian De Tomaso Automobile Company. Although its mid-engine configuration qualified it for 'exotic car' status, the De Tomaso Pantera cost far less than a comparable Ferrari or Lamborghini because of its relatively inexpensive Ford engine. The car now lives at the Petersen Automotive Museum. Leslie Kendall, Chief Curator of the museum explains the value of this Elvis-owned car by saying 'Unless somebody finds a gold-plated one that was driven by the Pope to victory at Le Mans, then it probably is the most valuable!'

The Cadillac Seville V8 automatic is believed to be the last car that Elvis bought for his own personal use and was driven by him the day before he died. Elvis had a CB radio installed so that he could communicate with the Graceland kitchen and put in his food order for his return. The car features a custom-built body by Fisher for Cadillac and Elvis chose the two-tone burgundy and silver paintwork. The car was given to Elvis' girlfriend Ginger Alden when he died and is now displayed at the National Motor Museum in Beaulieu, UK.

Tales of extreme decadence have become part of Elvis folklore, illustrated beautifully by his insatiable appetite for purchasing cars. During his lifetime it is estimated that Elvis bought over 270 cars, the majority of which were given to friends, family and occasionally total strangers. The purchasing of a new car became a therapeutic experience for Elvis – a well-deserved pick-me-up when life wore him down. 'You know, when some people get down and out, they go out and get drunk and forget it all. Me, I just go out and buy another car' Elvis once confessed. Priscilla added that if Elvis 'heard someone was sad or depressed, he loved to surprise them with a gift, usually a brand-new car'. Just as the style-conscious might update their wardrobe seasonally, Elvis added the latest models to his fleet as they were released. He purchased the cars spontaneously and the local Memphis dealerships grew accustomed to receiving calls from Elvis in the middle of the night, gratefully opening their gates so he could make an instant purchase.

'Impulsiveness was very much a feature of Elvis' personality. It was partly circumstantial, brought on by his unheralded success. His early life was very simple and on the edge of deprivation, so when he became successful and the world was his oyster, there were really no limits' observes Dr Peter Collett. 'There is a big 'Kar-Kulture' in America. Cars, more than clothes, are seen as a token of success, so within that context the most loving, generous expression of affection would be giving someone a car. Elvis was simply using the currency available, no doubt, in an extremely affectionate way' he adds.

This car was brought as part of one of Elvis' final, legendary Cadillac shopping sprees. The automobile is now owned by Elvis tribute artist Jeremy Pearce and can be hired for corporate events, with the incentive that you too can sit where The King once sat.

At 2am on 14th January 1976, Elvis went on a car-buying rampage whilst in Colorado on a skiing trip. He bought nine Cadillacs as gifts for his manager, friends' girlfriends and a few chosen acquaintances from the local police force. When an NBC television anchor-man reported on the shopping trip and joked that he would also like one, Elvis arranged for a brand new Cadillac Seville to be delivered to his studio the following morning. Even by Elvis' standards, it was a legendary shopping spree. Three months after the Colorado trip, Shirley Dieu (the girlfriend of Elvis' close friend Joe Esposito) upgraded the green Eldorado that Elvis had bought her for a baby blue version, making this officially the last Cadillac that Elvis purchased.

The tour bus used by Elvis' backing singers, J. D. Sumner and The Stamps. Elvis gave them a cheque for $25,000 to buy and refurbish the bus, on the condition that he could take it for a drive once it was completed. George Barris, who customised a Greyhound bus for Elvis' personal use, says that the star enjoyed being behind the wheel of a tour bus. 'He would want to cool off after recording all night and the way he did this was to drive the bus. He would drive the four-hour-long trip from Los Angeles to Vegas himself. I made him a special seat so that he could drive in comfort' says Barris. Even as Elvis became increasingly agoraphobic in later years, he continued to drive his autos himself. Elvis' cars and buses offered him a security bubble where he could venture into the world beyond Graceland's gates, while still feeling protected.

Named after Elvis' daughter Lisa Marie, his beloved personal plane was also nicknamed The Flying Graceland.

Elvis Planes

In 1975 Elvis bought a former Delta Air Lines passenger plane, which he christened the Lisa Marie. The Convair 880 Jet was bought for $250,000 and Elvis promptly spent $300,000 and seven months having it painstakingly refurbished, by a team in Texas who had also designed the interior of the presidential Air Force One plane. The original 110 passenger airline seats were taken out and replaced with a luxurious master bedroom, a deluxe sleeping area for his entourage, a lounge area and a conference room decorated with teak. Elvis' lavish en-suite bathroom featured a washbasin covered in flakes of 24k gold, a soap dish, towel rail imported from Spain and illuminated Hollywood lights framing the mirror. The chairs in the lounge area were made from leather, suede and velvet, and the seat belts throughout the plane were plated in real gold.

No expense was spared with refurbishing the Lisa Marie to Elvis' exacting requirements. Elvis was heavily involved with the interior design decisions, from the layout to the materials used throughout.

The on-board conference room with minibar.

In the two years that Elvis owned the Lisa Marie, it made over 200 flights, mostly transporting him to his concerts but occasionally taking a trip for pleasure. The plane became steeped in mythology when it carried Elvis on his famous 1,000-mile journey from Memphis to Denver in 1976, in search of the perfect sandwich. Nick Andurlakis, a chef at the Colorado Mine Company restaurant at the time, recalls that Elvis had visited the restaurant after performing at a concert locally and tried the Fool's Gold Loaf sandwich, made from peanut butter, jelly and bacon. 'When he left, Elvis said he would be back sometime for more of my sandwiches – well, you know people say things like that but you never really think it's going to happen' Andurlakis recollects. He was therefore amazed when Elvis put in a personal call to say he was firing up the Lisa Marie plane to fly to Denver, just to sample the sandwich again.

Contrary to the popular myth that the Fool's Gold Loaf trip was the extravagant whim of a bored superstar, Andurlakis says that the flight was an airborne celebration for Elvis' daughter, Lisa Marie, as it was her 8th birthday. 'Elvis said, "I want to fly out to Denver and I want a lot of the sandwiches you made for me, and whatever else you think we need". He said he wanted to have a birthday party for his young daughter in the air. Nobody ever really knew that story, but the reason he flew out here was to celebrate Lisa's birthday with her'. At 1.40 am on 1st February 1976, Elvis' plane had touched down in Denver and Andurlakis and his colleagues delivered the sandwiches to the special hangar, where Elvis and the group spent three hours enjoying the feast. They promptly flew back to Memphis without having left the airport – a trip that had cost an estimated $16,000. 'Lisa was with him and I got to meet her' Andurlakis remembers. 'I chatted to Elvis about his jewellery collection and he showed me a box of watches and jewellery that he travelled with. We also discussed Graceland and he said I had an open invitation to visit – he gave me the number for his bedroom phone and said he would send the plane out to get me. I didn't take him up on the offer as we had a busy restaurant and were working almost every day' Andurlakis recalls regretfully.

Elvis took another plane trip to Colorado with his daughter when he realised she had never seen snow. After Lisa Marie had a quick play in the snow, they headed back to Memphis for dinner.

Elvis also owned a smaller Lockheed Jetstar plane, named the Hound Dog II. It was bought in 1975 to transport Elvis to Texas, so he could closely follow the refurbishment of his Lisa Marie plane. Elvis paid almost $900,000 for the Hound Dog II, which could seat ten people and was flown by his personal pilot, Milo High. What the plane lacked in space, it made up for in style, with its distinctive leather seats in vibrant lime green and citrus yellow.

**The exterior of Elvis'
Hound Dog II plane.**

**Fresh and funky – the
interior of the Hound Dog
II plane.**

'I know what poverty is. I lived it for a long time…I am not ashamed of my background'

Elvis Presley.

Elvis Architecture

Shotgun to Social Housing – the Early Years

'Elvis Slept Here' the sign boasts, quite possibly with an element of truth. Elvis had spent much of his adult life either relentlessly touring throughout America or lodging in Hollywood. The houses that Elvis lived in during his lifetime span the extremes of American architecture – from a Southern shotgun shack, to one of the country's first social housing projects, nostalgic Colonial style mansions to cutting edge Modernist masterpieces.

In the early morning of 8th January 1935, Elvis Aaron Presley was born in a simple shack in Tupelo, Mississippi. His arrival followed the birth of his stillborn twin brother, Jesse Garon Presley. Elvis' father Vernon, Vernon's parents, a midwife, an unnamed friend and a doctor crowded into the small bedroom to assist with the difficult birth. The impoverished Presleys were unable to afford the $15 medical fee for Elvis' arrival and aftercare, so the county covered the cost. A more humble entry into the world would be hard to imagine, as the house that welcomed him was a single-width shotgun house, just one room wide and two rooms deep.

According to folklore, the shotgun house gained its name because if you fired a gun from the front porch of the house, the bullet would cruise through the house and come out the other side without hitting anything. This style of vernacular housing has a rich history and cultural binding to the Southern States, having gained popularity from the 1830s onwards, when it is commonly thought to have migrated to New Orleans via Afro-Haitian slaves. Following the American Civil War, both the working and middle classes favoured the shotgun as a solution to the housing crisis, as the cities were flooded with new arrivals. This shotgun offered a quick fix – it was relatively inexpensive, simple to construct and fitted neatly into narrow urban lots.

**The façade of Elvis' birthplace,
306 Old Saltillo Road, Tupelo.**

However, by the time Vernon Presley built his modest 15 by 30 foot house at the height of The Great Depression in 1934, the glory days of the shotgun were over and it had become a visual symbol of the impoverished Deep South. The shotgun shanty was now housing exclusively for the poor, typically built by sharecroppers on the landowner's property. True to form, the newlywed Vernon went to his landlord and borrowed the $180 needed for his first home, which he built with the help of his father Jesse and brother Vester. Self-building was still common at this time, with the majority of 1930s American housing being constructed either by the owner or a local contractor. Vernon, who was just 18 years of age, used tongue and groove boards that he left unpainted. The solid structure had certainly been built with a degree of skill, as it survived a tornado in 1936 that killed over 200 Tupelo residents and levelled out entire blocks of the city.

The wooden shack was one of nine similar houses, snugly lined up in a row on Old Saltillo Road in East Tupelo; an area considered to be the wrong side of the tracks. The Presley family had neither running water nor electricity, despite Tupelo residents being the first in Mississippi to have electricity, offered at a subsidised rate to improve rural living conditions. Their toilet was a shared wooden outhouse, which was standard in marginalised communities at that time. In keeping with the Southern practice, the house was elevated using stacks of bricks, allowing cooling air to flow around the structure and floodwater to pass under it. Chickens scratched around in the surrounding dirt yard, which was swept daily with a broom by Gladys. Twice weekly, the Presleys would meet with their neighbouring extended family to sing hymns on the porch. The communal living approach that the Presleys fostered at their shotgun house would continue to influence Elvis' lifestyle as an adult, as he was known for keeping an interwoven clique of family and friends close by at all times.

Shotgun living 'requires a different set of family ground rules', Professor Jay D. Edwards from the Louisiana State University observes. 'Some people complain about the lack of privacy. Everyone, including strangers and local guests, must pass through every bedroom in a single shotgun to get to the kitchen in the rear, where the real social life of the family goes on. Thus, the family always feels obligated to "make house" as they say in New Orleans, to keep it neat'. This is unlikely to have concerned Elvis' mother, who took pride in her role as homemaker. Perhaps it also helped that the Presleys had very little in the way of personal belongings to create clutter. Many years later, Vernon was to receive a call from the curator of the soon to be opened Elvis Presley Birthplace Museum, asking for a description of the original furnishings so they could be replicated. Vernon's baffled response was that due to their poverty there really wasn't much to speak of, and that at that time they had just been grateful to have a roof over their heads.

A replica of the outhouse that the Presleys would have shared with their neighbours and the members of the local Pentecostal Assembly of God Church, which the Presleys also attended. For sanitary reasons, outhouses were located away from the houses. The simple wooden structure had ventilation holes cut out of the door or sidewalls. It would have been chillingly cold in the winter months and have attracted insects in the summertime.

Unfortunately the Presleys' domestic stability was cut short when Vernon was jailed for eight months for allegedly forging a cheque. Gladys fell behind on the repayments, so she and her infant son were forced to leave their house and move in with her husband's family temporarily. Although the shotgun house had not been of Elvis' choosing, it continued to have a profound effect on him and was often used as a yardstick to measure the distance between where he had started and where he had at arrived at. In later years, Elvis was fond of driving the two-hour journey from his Graceland estate to his Tupelo birthplace, where he would sit in his car outside the shack and contemplate how a boy born with so little, now seemed to have too much of everything. His birthplace and Graceland visually represented the American Dream so concisely; as neatly as the shack could have fitted into Elvis' front room in his Graceland mansion – a comparison that Elvis himself would often make.

The Presleys had to share a bed in their cramped house.

As few people choose to visit grinding poverty in their leisure time, Elvis' birthplace and the surrounding grounds were gentrified before opening to the public as a historical museum. Tourism has become Mississippi's third largest business, fuelled by the musical heritage of its native sons who include Jimmie Rogers, Robert Johnson and of course, Elvis Presley.

The exterior of the shack has been whitewashed and floral wallpaper hung on the interior walls, which had been pasted with newspaper during the Presleys' tenure. Curtains, light bulbs, period furniture and luxuries such as a sewing machine and a child's highchair were added, with a swing on the porch and white picket fence at the back completing the nostalgic image of a rural idyll.

Elvis on the cusp, aged 12 years old and still living in Tupelo, Mississippi (1947). He was already experimenting with elongated collars and slick hair.

Having left the shotgun at the age of three, Elvis was to move fifteen more times during his childhood as his parents struggled to make ends meet with a series of fluid jobs – Gladys working as a sewing machine operator and Vernon at various times working as a sharecropper, truck driver, carpenter and painter. In 1948, when Elvis was thirteen, the family packed up their meagre belongings, leaving Tupelo and heading to Memphis in search of a better life. They found it the following year, when they were offered an apartment in Lauderdale Courts – one of America's first public housing projects, which aimed to showcase a new model of residential living for low-income communities. The Presleys had timed the move well, as the standard of social housing at that time was generally high, with President Franklin Roosevelt injecting billions of dollars into public works buildings, under his 'Works Progress Administration' scheme. For Lauderdale Courts, which replaced a former slum, The Memphis Housing Authority had teamed up with Joe Frazer Smith, a respected Mississippi-born architect who was also a scholar of early Southern buildings. Using a Georgian Colonial style, he organised the 449 apartments around neat, shared courtyards to create a tangible sense of community. The housing blocks did not reach above four storeys in height and the 26-acre development also boasted play parks, a recreation hall and a mall. As it was built during the days of segregation, Lauderdale Courts was housing exclusively for whites. Frazer Smith created a similar complex down the road called Dixie Homes for African American residents.

The corridor of Elvis' block at Lauderdale Courts is now home to a photomontage showing the young Presley family.

The exterior of Elvis' block at Lauderdale Courts. During the Presleys' tenancy, the residents were a close-knit community who shared a common vision of upward mobility and pride in their habitat. It was perhaps this congenial atmosphere that allowed Gladys to ask her neighbour's son to teach Elvis the basics on his guitar. Elvis would practise in the evenings, sitting on the narrow ledge outside his bedroom window, or out on the concrete steps at the entrance of his block. The complex fell on hard times and was almost demolished in the 1990s, but has now been refurbished for mixed-income housing and renamed Uptown Square Apartments. A swimming pool, fitness room and business centre have been added to the complex in recent years.

For a reasonable sum of $35 per month in rent, the Presleys now had a five-room home. Although the apartment was in need of repairs when the family arrived, it was a vast improvement on the Memphis boarding house that they were leaving behind, where they had shared a single room and cooked meals on a hot plate. Gladys' new kitchen featured a standard issued four-hob stove, Frigidaire, a shiny porcelain sink, drainer and room for a breakfast table and three chairs. She soon stocked up on Stanley Home Products utensils, bought at Tupperware parties that she would attend with her teenage son. Oak parquet flooring ran throughout the spacious living room, which also housed the family's telephone and radio and later a television set, which was still considered a luxury item at that time. The white tiled bathroom, with its freshly repainted porcelain tub, was next to Gladys and Vernon's bedroom. Perhaps to compensate for the fact that this was the first time in Elvis' life that he had his own bedroom, his parents gave their treasured son the larger room. Elvis could open his window and hear the freight trains racing past and sounding their horns late into the night, or if the wind was blowing in the right direction, the faint sound of music being enjoyed on Beale Street.

The Presleys'
kitchen.

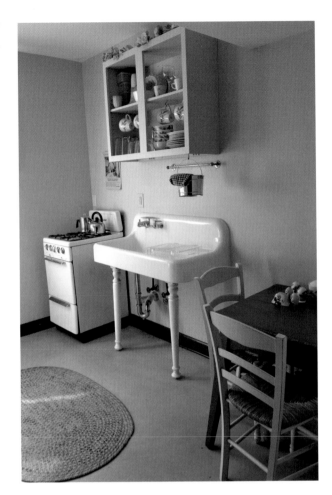

The Presleys'
living room.

Elvis' bedroom at Lauderdale Courts.

The Presleys' tiled bathroom.

A portrait of Elvis hanging
in his parents' bedroom.

Elvis' yearbook from high school.

Perhaps the single most significant aspect of Lauderdale Courts was its location and the exposure this offered Elvis. During these formative years the cultural heart of Memphis was right on Elvis' doorstep. Suddenly the record stores, the ostentatious clothing shops and blues sounds of Beale Street, the all-night gospel singings at the Ellis Auditorium, and the WMPS radio station where the Blackwood Brothers would perform, were within walking distance; all of which Elvis experienced and soaked up like a sponge. Who knows, perhaps if the Presleys had been housed elsewhere during this period, the distinctive elements that Elvis brought together in his music and style would have been different and may have produced another outcome altogether.

The Presleys had spent four contented years living in The Courts, but regrettably they were asked to leave in early 1953, as their household income had reached above the housing association threshold. The trio packed up their belongings and were on the road again, lodging in a series of rental homes for the next three years, until fame came calling and the 21-year-old Elvis could finally put down roots and buy his family their first home – a four-bedroom ranch house on Audubon Drive, in a quiet suburb of Memphis. Elvis paid $40,000 for the property and added an outdoor swimming pool, plus walls and gates to offer some privacy from the fans congregating at the front of the house. Elvis only spent 13 months at Audubon Drive but it provided a stepping-stone between the transient lifestyle of his childhood and the security and permanence that he was to find with the purchase of his next house, Graceland.

This telephone table with a green vinyl cushioned seat came from the Presleys' Audubon Drive home, which had been bought from the profits of Elvis' first national hit, *Heartbreak Hotel*. It was situated in the living room and would have been used by Gladys for her daily phone calls to her son while he was absent from the house with touring commitments.

Elvis' gramophone.

Baby, Let's Play House; Elvis and Graceland

Graceland is arguably one of the most significant American homes of the twentieth century. As a design archive, it offers an extensive catalogue of interior trends from the late 1950s through to the 70s, often in their purest and most authentic forms. Thematic rooms, meticulous colour scheming and the use of technology in the home are all indicative trends of the era. The house is a goldmine of creative ideas and offers a template for contemporary designers. Indeed Deborah Cavendish, Duchess of Devonshire, recently commented that 'There can be nowhere like Graceland – students of the decorative arts should see it as part of their education'.

Graceland is not only a site of design pedagogy and conservation, however, but also holds a mirror up to our present-day culture. When Elvis moved into his cherished home in the late 1950s it marked the starting point of our contemporary obsession with the domestic lives of the rich and famous. As Helen Kirwan-Taylor noted in *The Wall Street Journal*, 'Graceland was a precursor to the sort of lavish properties inhabited by today's footballers and oligarchs and splashed across magazine spreads'.

Over the years Graceland has experienced many incarnations – from an aristocratic family home, to a derelict, lonely mansion on the hill, then from the cherished home of the King of Rock and Roll, to finally becoming the second most visited home in America, beaten only by the White House.

The story of Graceland begins back in 1939, when the wealthy socialite Ruth Brown Moore and her doctor husband commissioned a two-storey Classical Revival residence on their land, about eight miles from Downtown Memphis. Local architects Merrill Ehrman and Max Furbringer were enlisted to create the design for the 10,000-square-foot mansion. Although the predominant focus of their practice was public buildings, they understood the aspirations that the Southern gentry had for their domestic spaces – offering them scaled-down versions of grandiose plantation owners' homes, which in turn were based on noble Greek temples that referenced a lost, idealised civilisation.

Graceland's famous music gates.

Graceland façade.

Blueprints of Graceland mansion, showing the front of the building, minus the white lion statues that Elvis added to flank the front steps. The rear of the building and architectural details such as the façade columns and the white staircase that leads up to Elvis' bedroom can be seen in the bottom image.

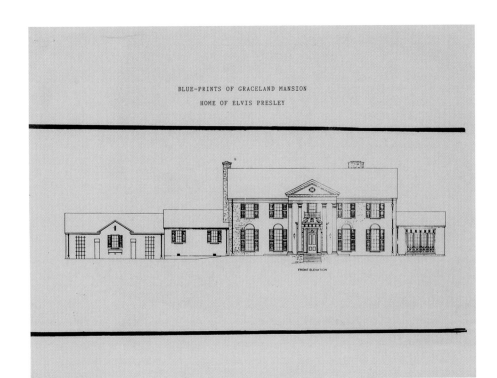

BLUE-PRINTS OF GRACELAND MANSION
HOME OF ELVIS PRESLEY

FRONT ELEVATION

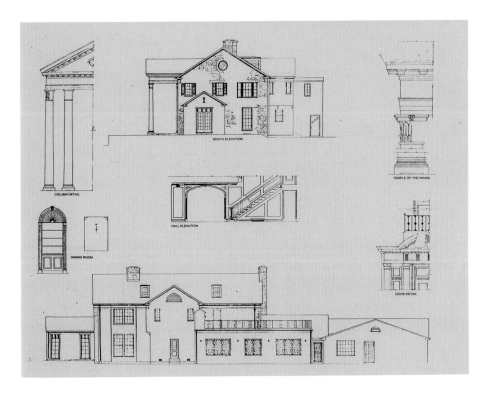

COLUMN DETAIL

SOUTH ELEVATION

TEMPLE OF THE WINDS

HALL ELEVATION

DINING ROOM

DOOR DETAIL

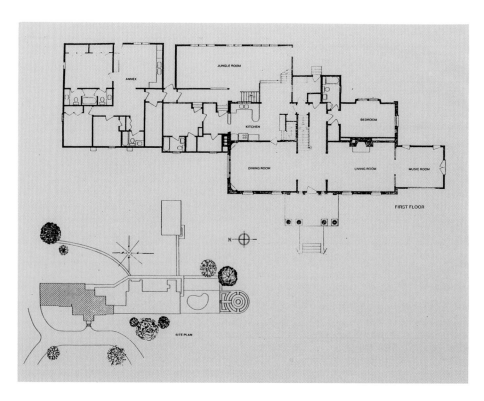

FIRST FLOOR

SITE PLAN

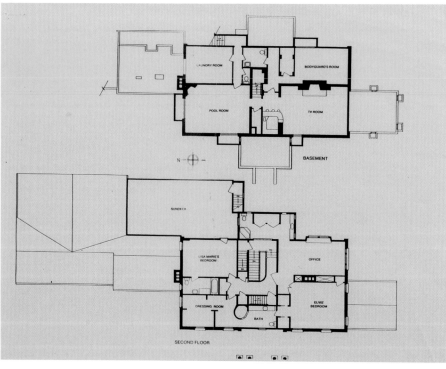

BASEMENT

SECOND FLOOR

172

The top image shows the ground floor of Graceland, which is open to the public. Elvis' parents' bedroom is on the far right and the Jungle Room can be seen at the back of the building. Much of the basement floor, seen on the plan below, is also part of the public tour. The bottom image shows the layout of the elusive second floor of Graceland, which is closed off to the public. The floor plan includes Elvis' master bedroom, his daughter Lisa Marie's bedroom and a wardrobe room, where Elvis kept a circular white fur bed with a built-in television overhead. Elvis kept his elaborate stage costumes in this room, hung on heavy-duty iron rods to support their weight. In Elvis' bedroom, he kept a closed circuit TV monitor where he could observe what was happening within the house and at Graceland's front gates.

For the façade of Graceland, a mood of restrained splendour was attempted with a classical full-height portico supported by Corinthian columns which reference the 'Tower of the Winds' marble clock-tower in Athens, with a distinctive single ring of acanthus leaves surrounding a row of palm leaves. The Tower of the Winds column had become a popular addition at the front of houses, as it was cheaper to create than a full Greek Corinthian capital but still offered a stately appearance. The architects Ehrman and Furbringer would most likely have used the published works of Renaissance authorities such as Serlio and Palladio for researching and incorporating Grecian elements into the design of Graceland. Inside, the house had been decorated in the Colonial Revival style, with wood panelling painted in oyster white, Chinese and European teakwood furniture and antique Aubusson rugs. They christened the house Graceland after Ruth's aunt Grace, who had originally owned the land.

Graceland would almost certainly have remained an upper class residence had fate not dealt its hand in 1957, when the recently divorced Mrs Brown Moore sold the vacant house and estate to the Presley family for just over $100,000. At just 22 years of age, Elvis had initially been uncertain that he could maintain such an extensive mansion and grounds, but fellow showman Liberace provided the verbal encouragement he needed to sign the contract. Before the ink had dried, the local media were already speculating on Elvis' design schemes. 'In Memphis, at least, it was front-page news' said George Golden, a local interior designer who worked on Graceland. 'There were big headlines everywhere declaring "Elvis Presley Buys Graceland".' Once the news had become national, people from across America flocked to Graceland to catch a glimpse of Elvis' home. 'It was truly unbelievable, seeing these cars from other states driving by just to get a look at this old house that had been sitting there for years' Golden recalls. 'It was a sideshow out there. People were lined up against the fence, picking grass and sticking it between the pages of books. Some people were even kissing the ground'.

Those who were curious to know what was happening within Graceland's walls were not kept in the dark for long. In the same month that Elvis bought Graceland, he invited local journalists over to tour the property and discuss his plans for the house, which included a black bedroom suite with white leather trim and a mirror running along the length of the room. He also spoke of his desire for a hi-fi system in every room and a fenced-off space for his mother to keep chickens on the grounds. That such a level of interest was shown in how a male singer decorates his family home was, and still is, quite extraordinary.

Once Elvis had acquired Graceland, the renovations started almost immediately, with the Presleys spending a staggering half a million dollars on the house in the first six months alone. When he returned to Hollywood to film *Jailhouse Rock*, Elvis left his mother and the decorating team from Goldsmith's department store in Memphis to work to his specific brief. George Golden, who had recently designed Sun Records mogul Sam Phillips' house, was also employed sporadically over the next two years to work on Graceland's interiors. At the time, Golden was one of only three interior designers in the Memphis area, and he used an unusual advertising gimmick of driving a flatbed truck around town, showcasing scaled-down room sets.

The Living Room at Graceland, dressed for the festive season. At the far end of the photo, framed by the peacock stained glass panels, is The Music Room. Elvis used this space for informal jam sessions and karate demonstrations. The piano that currently resides at Graceland is a black Story & Clark model, which Elvis had installed at the mansion in the 1970s.

In his absence, Gladys made subtle tweaks to her son's design blueprint, such as swapping deep purple for a Dresden blue colour and discarding the painted clouds and twinkling lights in the entranceway – an idea borrowed from Liberace. Nevertheless, Elvis' grand scheme for a private paradise was coming to life. The white walls were trimmed with cornices decorated with gold-leaf gilding, thick white shag pile carpeting ran throughout the ground floor and heavy, blue velvet drapes hung at the windows – switched to red for the festive season. A boundary wall and embellished gates were installed, featuring life-sized, wrought iron Elvis figures surrounded by musical notes, framing the view up to the mansion and acting as a Presley suit of arms. A high-tech soda fountain and a modest-sized kidney-shaped swimming pool were also swiftly added. Graceland's disciplined colour schemes were in keeping with the ideals of prominent designers of the time such as Billy Baldwin or William Pahlmann, who introduced the deep, romantic colours that swept through houses at the end of the decade. By the end of the 1950s, Elvis had rapidly acquired the material comforts of the era – he was now the proud owner of a sprawling, suburban family house filled with the latest gadgetry including an outdoor jukebox and a mixer at each end of the kitchen, so his mother would not have to walk far – and was on his way towards turning the American Dream into a reality.

During his Hollywood years Elvis had kept a pet chimpanzee named Scatter, who was dressed up in miniature outfits and carried around like a baby. The mischievous chimp's behaviour eventually became uncontrollable and he was sent back to Graceland and rehoused in an air-conditioned cage at the back of the mansion. After Scatter died of natural causes, Elvis installed a number of porcelain monkey statues at Graceland. This monkey duo once resided in the dining room, and a similar ornament can still be found crouching on the mirrored coffee table of Graceland's TV room.

A replica of Elvis' cream leather sofa can be found at the Graceland Randers museum in Denmark.

However, by the 1960s, the suburban ideals of the previous decade were being renounced in favour of a more adventurous, youth-orientated vision. It was a style revolution with which both Elvis and Graceland became increasingly out of touch. The American Modern design of the 1950s had given way to experimental plastic furniture from Italy, psychedelic British pattern design, as used by influential designers such as David Hicks, and simple Scandinavian furniture – all of which made little impact on the interiors of Elvis' home. Neither did the trend for minimalism, spearheaded by designers such as Ward Bennett and Nicos Zographos, who stripped back ornamentation to create clean, white cubed rooms. Perhaps at first glance, Graceland's heavy drapery, colour matching and grandiose chandeliers could be compared to the opulent style favoured by designers such as Mark Hampton and Mario Buatta, who had resisted ultra-modernism, instead favouring a reduplicated archival approach that was influenced by the stately homes of Europe. However, an important criterion for these star-designers was their use of genuine antique furniture, signifying the owner's social prominence. In contrast, the furniture at Graceland was mainly bought from moderately priced local department stores. Elvis would explain that his aversion to antiques was rooted in the poverty of his childhood – he had been around enough old stuff to last a lifetime.

177

Elvis did manage, however, to hit on a number of eminent 1960s interior trends – most notably the move towards elongated furniture (Elvis installed a 15-foot long custom-made couch and 10-foot long table in the living room, to surreal effect) and an interest in spirituality, influenced by the emerging hippie movement. By the mid-1960s Elvis had become increasingly discontented with his film career and had turned his mind towards esoteric texts. He made frequent visits to the Self-Realization Fellowship Lake Shrine in California; a site of lush gardens, waterfalls and lakes where a portion of Mahatma Gandhi's ashes are held. Wanting to create a similar space at Graceland for quiet contemplation, Elvis commissioned the local builder Bernard Grenadier to design a tranquil space that incorporated the existing semi-circular pergola of Ionic columns. A wall of Mexican brickwork with Spanish stained glass windows was added, along with a circular pool with fountain jets, landscaped flowerbeds and speakers that were wired up to the sound system in the house. Unbeknown to Elvis at the time of the Meditation Garden's construction, it would later become his final resting place, after his body was returned to Graceland following safety concerns at the cemetery where he had initially been buried.

The mid-60s also saw Elvis become a forerunner for the contemporary phenomenon of the self-revealing celebrity, when he invited *Mid-South Magazine* into his home to photograph him posing in various rooms throughout the property – strumming a guitar in the living room as he reclined on the deluxe sofa, or playing a snow-white grand piano in the music room. Elvis and Graceland were to become so interchangeable that the cover of the 1974 album *Elvis Recorded Live on Stage in Memphis* featured a simple photo of the front of the mansion, replacing the conventional pop star portrait. Long before Graceland opened its doors for tours, it was already in the public consciousness through photos and even musical recordings that took place in his domestic space.

What to give the man who has everything? Priscilla must have pondered on her one-year wedding anniversary. She found the answer by secretly having Elvis' favourite piano painted in dazzling gold leaf. Elvis had originally bought this handsome Kimball piano, previously owned by Memphis' Dixon-Myers concert Hall, in 1955 at an auction. After Priscilla applied the Midas touch to the baby grand piano, it became the focal point of Graceland's music room in the late 1960s. The top right image shows the piano in situ at Graceland – illuminated in the distance and evocative of the youthful Elvis in his dazzling gold suit.

A monogrammed Wallace Baroque silver-plated punchbowl, tray and cup set that Elvis purchased in 1960. The tray is engraved with a P for Presley and was given by Elvis to his father Vernon when he married his second wife, Dee Stanley, much to Elvis' disapproval. Wallace Silver was responsible for introducing German silver into the American market, becoming a prominent name in the silver industry.

Rarely has such synergy between a celebrity and their home occurred – made even more revealing by the fact that Elvis had full ownership of the design decisions and treated Graceland as an outlet for his creativity. Elvis took pleasure in researching his latest interior projects – for example, he covered the walls of his billiard room with 320 metres of pleated fabric after finding inspiration in a picture that he had found of a traditional eighteenth-century billiard room. When it was decided that an outhouse was no longer needed, Elvis was behind the wheel of the bulldozer, tearing it down as his friends cheered him on. Even Priscilla Presley, who lived at Graceland for over a decade, was the first to admit that Elvis had carte blanche over the décor and that her input was limited to changing the drapes seasonally.

By the beginning of the 1970s, Graceland's interiors fell back into fashion, as the design arbiters turned their backs on Modernism and embraced extreme ornamentation and pluralism – both areas that were an easy fit with Elvis' aesthetic values. Graceland's swan song came in 1974, three years before Elvis' death, when he embarked on a large-scale decorating binge, assisted by his then girlfriend Linda Thompson and a young interior design student called Bill Eubanks. The resulting 'Red Phase' saw the ground floor of the house transformed into a sea of red shag pile carpeting, crimson satin drapes laced with gold tassels, teamed with white Mongolian fur cushions and rugs, and gold gilt–edged mirrors. A black-velvet painting adorned with sparkling fairy lights had been hung by the fireplace, a transparent statue of a naked woman revolved under a waterfall of plastic beads, while trinkets and ostrich feathers jostled for space in the glass cabinets. There was hardly an inch of space that wasn't provocative. It was a fantastical setting, which the design journalist Dominic Lutyens, co-author of the *70s Style & Design* tome, notes 'One could have imagined being the interior of the home of a Disney princess'.

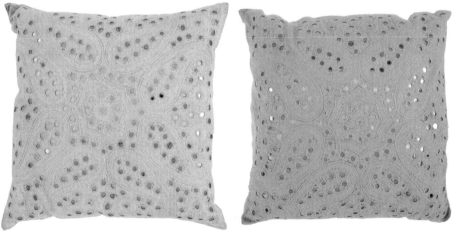

These mirrored cushions were introduced into Graceland's TV room and living room as part of the 1974 redecorations.

In the basement, the TV room became a homage to 1970s pop-meets-Art Deco, with a striking colour palette of canary yellow, white and navy and a mirrored ceiling. A large cloud and lightning motif was painted across the wall, symbolising Elvis' motto 'TCB', in a flash. The interior was 'a la mode when it was created in 1974', according to Dominic Lutyens. 'The 70s saw a big revival of Art Deco, conveyed here by the mural and also by the chocolate brown elements and the velvety-looking sofas and pouffes'. Three television sets are mounted into the far wall – an idea that Elvis took from President Lyndon Johnson who watched all three news broadcasts simultaneously. 'The room reflects an interest in the latest technology which was an obsession in the 1970s, even though the decade also saw a major backlash against technology and consumerism, spearheaded by the hippie movement. People often had mirrored ceilings above their beds in the 1970s – it seems to have been seen as rather racy at the time' Lutyens observes. Overlooking the disco-groovy décor is a white china monkey statue, crouching on a mirrored coffee table, a style of ornament that Lutyens notes was fashionable 'among the rich and haute-bourgeois' at the time.

In keeping with the era's yearning for rustic, farmhouse-inspired interiors, Graceland's kitchen is of the Country Vernacular style, with mahogany panelled cabinets and walls. Imitation Tiffany lightshades, with stained glass patterns of fruit and vegetables hang from the ceiling, the sink is a modish avocado green colour and a dishwasher is discreetly veiled under a counter.

Graceland's 1974 renovations had also witnessed the creation of the notorious Polynesian themed Jungle Room. Green shag pile carpeting covers both the floor and ceiling, a waterfall seeps down the fake brickwork of the far wall, and carved wooden furniture competes with fake fur upholstery. Hanging macramé plant holders are positioned around the room, mirroring the belts that Elvis had incorporated into his stage-wear at the time – further blurring the boundaries between reality and the stage set, between the interior and exterior of both the icon Elvis and Graceland. Although in many ways the Jungle Room is a less carefully coiffured environment than is to be seen in the rest of the house, it is nonetheless heavily over-constructed and thematic. Despite its artificiality there is an attempt at something organic and natural, although possibly not a successful one, as the pretence of the natural makes the room's artificiality all the more apparent.

The Jungle Room showcases the 1970s 'back-to-nature' trend, with its grass-like carpeting, indoor houseplants and wood-panelled walls. The room's centre piece – an organic looking coffee table – would have been considered very contemporary, sharing a similarity with the designs of the Japanese-born, American based-designer George Nakashima, 'who was part of the US Studio or Art Furniture Movement. His tables were often made of cross sections of tree trunks and were popular with arty, avant-garde types' Lutyens says. The Polynesian-inspired décor also references Hawaii, where Elvis had enjoyed spending time on vacation and filming, as well as the interiors of bars such as Trader Vic's and Don the Beachcomber, which became fashionable in the 60s as Americans flocked to bamboo bars and oceanic-inspired fast-food joints in their leisure time. 'Arguably the décor is also a bit 1950s Hollywood too, perhaps inspired by the Tarzan movies' Lutyens notes, making a comparison with the 'Jungle Rock' or 'Caveman' themed rooms at the celebrated Madonna Inn Motel in California, which opened at the end of the 1950s.

The Jungle Room at Graceland Mansion.

In homage to his karate nickname, Mr Tiger, Elvis kept a number of tiger figurines in his home. This 19-inch-long ceramic model was made in Italy and resided at Graceland during the 1970s.

If legend is to be believed, then the jungle room is the only room at Graceland to be considered truly kitsch. Apparently Elvis had bought the entire window display from Donald's furniture store in Memphis (who also provided the furnishings for the red velvet phase) as a spontaneous gag, after his father Vernon complained about the ugly furniture he had just seen Downtown. That Elvis might have been in-on-the-joke, using an element of tongue-in-cheek irony, positions the jungle room firmly within the knowing quotation marks of kitsch. The jungle room essentially allows us to laugh with Elvis, rather than at him – perhaps another contributing factor as to why it was allowed to stay, while the naïve camp of the red phase was later eliminated.

Elvis' jungle room telephone, which is now exhibited at Graceland Randers in Denmark.

Throughout his 20-year occupancy, Elvis had approached the decoration of Graceland in much the same way as he created his music or composed his wardrobe. He brought together a bricolage of styles and influences – from the Modern Baroque approach favoured by plush hotels, to theatrical Hollywood film sets; from exotic Polynesian tiki bars, to the maternal comfort of an all-American suburban ranch. The interiors became a pastiche of styles and eras; with Elvis treating each room as its own theatrical stage-set, showing little concern for creating a coherent vision that ran throughout the house.

However, what is not made immediately clear to the present-day Graceland visitor is that the house that they see before them is actually a post-mortem reconstruction. After Elvis passed away in 1977, his former wife Priscilla founded Elvis Presley Enterprises as the only way to preserve Elvis' beloved house on the diminishing inheritance, unveiling Graceland to the public in 1982. Prior to the opening, Priscilla had raided the attic and storage for furnishings previously belonging to the house in the late 1950s and 60s period and restored the ground floor rooms to a more palatable blue, cream and gold colour scheme. With a sleight of hand the red decor, which the biographer Albert Goldman had compared to a 'whore-house' had vanished, erasing both the memory of Elvis' later excesses and any changes that successive girlfriends such as Linda and Ginger had made to the house. Priscilla had skilfully restored both Graceland and Elvis' image to its former glory and her vision was a truly post-modern one – equally valuing the real and fake, past and present. The repackaging of the majority of the house was in fact the repackaging of Elvis as a brand, making the experience of Graceland an interpretation of history – a hyper-real, larger than life representation.

This bronze statue of a male faun had been part of Graceland's décor during the late 1960s, but was not chosen to be on display when the house opened to the public. 'The statuette is based on ancient sculpture and is not particularly indicative of decorative art in the late 1960s-early 70s, when Elvis bought it' comments Jim Steele, Rock Music Expert at Heritage Auctions. 'This is just speculation, but while Elvis may have appreciated ancient sculpture, he knew he wasn't buying "Art" when he purchased the statuette. The piece doesn't appear to be of high quality, or particularly valuable – except of course via its association with Elvis, which is the only reason it fetched thousands in our auction' he observes.

Although parts of Graceland have undoubtedly been gentrified, the house continues to be ridiculed as the naïve folly of the newly rich, or as Hugh Merrill describes it – 'Presley's plantation of bad taste'. It should be noted that Elvis could have easily afforded the services of a celebrated interior designer such as Sister Parish, the doyenne of American interior design. Parish had refurbished the White House for the President and Mrs Kennedy in 1961, using a scheme that united federal furniture, flowered chintz and furnishings from eighteenth-century France in a self-assured manner. Rather than buying into Parish's seductive notions of low-key privilege, Elvis instead chose to either design the rooms himself or employ provincial designers and builders. While on one level Graceland had grand aspirations – the classical façade, the gold piano and the indoor waterfall – in comparison to our modern-day expectations of luxury, Graceland appears strikingly modest in both size and scope. We are now accustomed to stories of the super-rich and their vast, regal stately homes, private zoos, multiple heli-pads and indoor swimming pools, in-house spas and mega-yachts. Perhaps the disparaging Graceland visitor feels a sense of frustration at Elvis' refusal to use his wealth to elevate his social status, or as columnist John Harris commented, that Elvis 'never quite transcended the walled-in horizons of the white Southern poor' and remained faithful to his roots.

Yet to dismiss Graceland in terms of taste or class is to overlook the beauty that lies hidden within the eclectic mish-mash of the house. The interiors may laugh in the face of the aesthetic restraint deplored by design experts such as Frank Alvah Parsons, but they are a visual celebration of Elvis' impulsive nature, an unbridled showcase of self-expression and individuality. It is a house that lifts the curtain not only on Elvis Presley the superstar; it also exposes the aesthetic and material aspirations of the wider culture that spawned him.

'Once we started driving into Palm Springs, there was a calmness that took over. I always loved that feeling; we really needed that at the time'.

Priscilla Presley

The House of Tomorrow – Elvis' Honeymoon Hideaway

Singing the Hawaiian Wedding Song from his hit movie *Blue Hawaii*, Elvis carried his elated bride Priscilla over the threshold of 1350 Ladera Circle in Palm Springs, the stylish house that was to become their honeymoon retreat. Hoping to find a sanctuary away from the glare of Hollywood, Elvis had been leasing the estate since the previous September. He and Priscilla had become so enamoured with the residence that they had originally planned to hold their wedding ceremony around the pool, but the idea was revoked when their neighbour, the notorious gossip columnist Rona Barrett, got wind of the plan and leaked the news on her nightly television broadcast. Instead, the couple settled for a clandestine dash to Las Vegas on 1st May 1967, where they were legally married in a frenzied ceremony at the Aladdin Resort & Casino on The Strip. Frank Sinatra's private jet whisked the newlyweds back to the house, now commonly referred to as the 'Honeymoon Hideaway', so that they could settle in for domestic life together.

Elvis' manager, Colonel Tom Parker, had a house in Palm Springs and encouraged his client to spend more time in the area. He hoped that away from the many temptations that Elvis seemed drawn towards, a new more wholesome chapter in the entertainer's life could unfold. For a while, at least, the strategy seemed to be working. It is believed that Elvis started planning the 1968 *Comeback Special* while staying at the house, and also that his daughter Lisa Marie was conceived at the Honeymoon Hideaway.

The Presleys fitted into Palm Springs with ease – this was after all an elite playground that had been welcoming the rich and famous since the 1920s. Liberace, Greta Garbo, and Frank Sinatra were just a few of the high profile stars attracted to the lifestyle of recreation, glamour and luxury that Palm Springs seemed to offer.

The area had also become a mecca for avant-garde architecture, spearheaded by the introduction of Modernism in the 1920s with the opening of the Oasis Hotel by Lloyd Wright, eldest son of Frank Lloyd Wright. Talented architects such as Albert Frey, Richard Neutra and Donald Wexler followed, creating sleek, modern buildings that responded to the Coachella Valley desert surroundings. Palm Springs was soon boasting the highest concentration of mid-century modernist architecture in America.

Although Palm Springs was open-minded to unusual and innovative architecture, it was the arrival of father and son developers, George and Robert Alexander that made Modernism accessible to all. The Alexander Construction Company built 2,200 homes in the area between 1955 and 1965, doubling the size of Palm Springs and changing its aesthetic character beyond recognition. Complexes of starter homes and tracts of affordable second homes for the middle classes were constructed. The introduction of air-conditioning suddenly opened up the possibility of year-round desert living and the houses became an instant success. Architects Dan Palmer and William Krisel designed the majority of the Alexander homes. Both the young architects were graduates of the University of Southern California Architecture School and were heavily influenced by the designs of Frank Lloyd Wright. The duo managed throughout their careers to bring Modernism to the masses with great success, designing over 30,000 homes throughout Southern California.

The Alexanders soon progressed to building larger mansions as weekend retreats for the 'New Hollywood Set'. Dean Martin and Marilyn Monroe each bought an Alexander house in the Las Palmas area, which was also the neighbourhood of Rat Pack leader Frank

Sinatra. In 1960 the Alexanders spent $300,000 building a striking Las Palmas show-house, which Robert Alexander and his wife Helene became so fond of they decided to make it their family home. The four-bedroom house was a showcase of indoor/outdoor living, with floor to ceiling windows offering panoramic views across the mountains and valley. Peanut brittle stonework was used throughout the interior and exterior to create coherence. There was not a square room in the entire house, as it had been designed around four concentric circles, separated over three floors. The five bathrooms boasted Jacuzzi tubs and walk-in wardrobes, while the kitchen featured a futuristic circular island with no fewer than six cooking hobs. At the front of the house, the raised, curved master bedroom jutted out, with high wrap-around windows, and at the back of the house was a tennis court, waterfall and fruit orchard.

1350 Ladera Circle was soon labelled the 'House of Tomorrow' after it and the Alexander family's glamorous lifestyle were showcased in an eight-page feature in *Look* magazine in 1962. Tragically, the dream came to an end in 1965, when George and Robert Alexander and their wives were killed in a plane crash. The local community, of which the prolific Alexanders had become the heart, went into shock and their deaths heralded the end of an era in Palm Springs' design history.

The following year, the pioneering Modernist home was leased to Elvis for an annual fee of $21,000. Presley biographer Peter Guralnick observes that in Palm Springs Elvis was surrounded by Tinseltown's elite and 'it might have seemed as if Elvis was at last joining the Hollywood establishment'. But Elvis' reclusive lifestyle, surrounded by his close-knit entourage, continued in much the same as way as it had operated in Los Angeles or Memphis. 'Indeed, he appeared more comfortable with the policemen who worked the security detail at his house or the air-conditioning servicemen who installed a powerful hotel-sized unit to keep the temperature at the meat-locker chill that Elvis preferred, than he did with the movie-town high society all around him' Guralnick notes.

The façade of 1350
Ladera Circle,
Palm Springs,
California.

One of the Presleys' neighbours – Mr Rex, a 100-ton Tyrannosaurus Rex created by the portrait artist Claude K. Bell in the 1960s to attract customers to his Wheel Inn Café in Cabazon, West of Palm Springs.

An example of one of the popular Alexander houses that changed the face of Palm Springs during the mid-twentieth century.

The sunken living room of 1350 Ladera Circle, with peanut brittle wall and a 64-foot built-in banquette sofa.

Elvis gave up the lease on 1350 Ladera Circle after one year, but continued to spend time in Palm Springs. In 1970, he purchased the house now dubbed 'Graceland West' in the exclusive Little Tuscany area and kept it as a weekend retreat until his death in 1977. The house was designed by Albert Frey, the father of Desert Modern architecture who was celebrated for his ability to integrate his buildings with the surrounding landscape. The five-bedroom house became unpopular with Priscilla after she allegedly found her husband and a professional cheerleading squad in the outdoor hot tub and following their 1973 divorce, Graceland West was to become a glorified bachelor pad for Elvis and his friends.

Elvis' old stomping ground, Palm Springs, with the San Jacinto Mountains as a backdrop.

Although Elvis may have lived in Palm Springs' Modernist masterpieces, the ideals attached to them – transparency, simplicity and the ability to explore the world in new ways, did not seem to have made a lasting impact on Elvis' lifestyle. However, for a moment in time the Honeymoon Hideaway had managed to be the elegant decompression chamber that the Presleys craved. As Priscilla recounted to *Architectural Digest* magazine, 'that was our getaway house. Once we started driving into Palm Springs, there was a calmness that took over. I always loved that feeling; we really needed that at the time'.

Elvis' Legacy

Elvis' career and personal style were bookended by sheer brilliance. In the mid-1950s, Elvis Presley managed to singlehandedly change the way that America, and much of the world beyond, dressed. From his clothing to his hair and home, he wrote the rulebook on how to use cultural appropriation with panache. As a master of reinvention, he shape-shifted into a dapper Hollywood leading man in the 1960s and, just as others were writing him off as irrelevant, Elvis set the record straight with the legendary *'68 Comeback Special*. The pure drama of the subsequent Las Vegas era opened the floodgates for a wave of androgynous glam rockers, leather-clad punk rockers, and attention-grabbing male peacocks.

Certain aspects of Elvis' lifestyle were ahead of the curve. He had a fondness for eclectic and kitsch interiors before the Postmodernism movement had truly taken hold. Elvis was also devoted to Southern-style cooking, decades before bearded hipsters would flock to cosmopolitan restaurants to sample it. It is, however, in the worlds of fashion and entertainment that Elvis continues to have the most tangible and direct influence.

'There isn't a costume designer alive who hasn't been inspired by Elvis' acknowledges Deborah Nadoolman Landis, the regarded designer who created Michael Jackson's iconic *Thriller* costume and the wardrobes for *Indiana Jones and the Raiders of the Lost Ark*. She is, however, quick to note that although Elvis' style was very distinctive, he is also part of a larger continuum of showmen and women. Having been influenced by the theatricality of performers such as the great Liberace, Elvis in turn inspired a subsequent generation of style icons that bring us up to the present day. 'What do we ultimately have to work with as costume designers? Silhouette, colour and reflection. Elvis was able to harness all of these but he certainly wasn't the first person to do this. He is part of a long tradition of performers who use clothing as a tool – Michael Jackson, Madonna and Lady Gaga have all done this since'. For Nadoolman Landis, Elvis' style bequest was showing men how to power dress. 'Elvis' 1970s stage-wear was almost a military look and the high collar was incredibly powerful. This is what he's remembered for' she states.

For Patricia Fields, fashion stylist for the hit television show *Sex and the City,* Elvis' lasting legacy was the freedom of expression that he initiated. Nicknamed 'The Great Seducer', Elvis' gyrating stage act was considered so sexual that his 1957 appearance on the Ed Sullivan Show was censored from the waist down. By challenging the social and moral values of his era, Elvis paved the way for erotically charged pop videos and stage acts that have since become customary. 'Elvis made the girls scream and he made sexy cool. That is why he is The King' Fields observes.

Barely a fashion season passes without at least a handful of designers tapping into the early Elvis rockabilly style. Alex Bilmes, editor of *Esquire* magazine, recognises that Presley's style heritage has influenced contemporary musicians as much as everyday street wear. 'Elvis' influence on men's style is incalculable. He is one of a handful of icons of mid-century Americana and you can still see his legacy everywhere. For example, Alex Turner of the Arctic Monkeys is channelling the *'68 Comeback Special* even when he's just popping to the shops for cigarettes' Bilmes comments. 'Elvis' legacy can also be seen in the enduring appeal of jeans and jackets: that indefinable but instantly recognisable point where preppy meets rocker meets work wear meets tailoring' Bilmes concludes.

Elvis may have dipped in and out of fashion throughout his career, but he always retained his natural style. All that Elvis was – from his fondness for camp interiors to his commitment to Southern home cooking, from his pastiche outfits to his theatrical shopping trips, was an uncompromising expression of his unique identity – now that's true style!

A loosely fitting, plaid sports jacket, teamed with a dress shirt and black trousers, became an instantly recognisable signature style worn by the youthful Elvis. Although Elvis bought his distinctive sports jackets from Lansky Bros. in Memphis, this modern version is from the Italian house of Kiton, creators of the world's most expensive suits.

The Italian tailoring expert Luca Rubinacci pays homage to break-through Elvis in these boldly coloured zoot pants and loafers.

Liberace may have worn it first, and Michael Jackson and Justin Bieber since, but Elvis still remains the most famous star to step out in a dazzling gold suit. This recent reincarnation was sent down the runway by the Italian fashion house Costume National.

Elvis helped in liberating men to wear
clothing that previously had been
considered exclusively for females.
This included wearing bubble-gum pink
in the 1950s and floral, Hawaiian prints
in the 1960s. This stylised, floral print
sweater is by the avant-garde British
menswear label Casely-Hayford.

Elvis understood the power of attention-grabbing white stage-wear, memorably using it for the tailored suit worn for the *'68 Comeback Special*. The high-street retailer H&M created a similar, Southern-plantation-style suit for their eco-conscious collection in 2013.

The French couture house Balmain combined the shiny black leather of Elvis' '68 costume with the jumpsuit silhouette of his later stage-wear for their Spring/Summer 2014 collection. Since Elvis wore the iconic *Comeback Special* costume, black leather stage-wear has become a tried-and-tested formula for entertainers looking to shed their former image like a skin, and replace it with some rock 'n' roll authority.

Ashley Williams' debut collection at London Fashion Week took early Elvis as its inspiration. Williams experimented with double-denim, cigarette pants, teddy bear bags and shift dresses printed with Elvis' portrait. The nostalgic, Americana collection also featured the embroidered catchphrase 'My heart belongs to Elvis Presley'.

Bibliography

Chapter 1

Lansky, Bernard. *Lansky Brothers: Clothier to the King*. Beckon Books, Nashville. 2010.

Orbison, Roy quoted in *Last Train to Memphis* by Guralnick, Peter. Little Brown and Company, UK. 1994.

Hilfiger, Tommy quoted in the New York Times. 'Hidden for Years at Graceland, His Clothes Have Left the Building' by Guy Trebay. Published 16th November, 2003.

Esquire Magazine UK: Collector's Issue: Icons of Style. February 2015.

Presley, Elvis quoted in *Elvis Presley in Hollywood: Celluloid Sell-Out* by Gerry McLafferty, Robert Hale Limited, London. 1989.

Head, Edith. *Edith Head's Hollywood*, by Edith Head & Paddy Calistro, E. P. Dutton, Inc., New York. 1983.

O'Toole, Peter. 'Peter O'Toole: 20 Best Quotes. The Telegraph'. 16th December 2013.

Knowles, Beyoncé. *Elvis: Viva Las Vegas* documentary. Directed by Scott Floyd Lochmus. ABC America. 18th September 2007.

Nixon, Richard. Quoted in *What Jefferson Read, Ike Watched and Obama Tweeted: 200 Years of Popular Culture in the Whitehouse* by Tevi Troy. Regency Publishing, Washington. 2013.

Aquilina Ross, Geoffrey. *The Day of the Peacock: Style for Men 1963–1973*. V & A Publishing, London. 2011.

Chase, Chris. 'Like a Prince from Another Planet'. *The New York Times*. 18th June, 1972.

Belew, Bill. 'Designer was called 'Man who dressed The King' Obituaries'. *Los Angeles Times.* 17th January 2008.

Beaulieu Presley, Priscilla. *Elvis and Me.* Arrow Books, London. 1986.

Chapter 3

Presley, Elvis quoted in *The Ultimate Elvis* by Patricia Jobe Pierce. Simon & Schuster, New York. 1994.

Rooks, Nancy. 'Nancy Rooks Interview'. famousinterview.ca. (12th November 2013).

Lawson, Nigella. *Nigella Bites.* Chatto & Windus, London. 2001.

Chapter 4

Presley, Elvis quoted in *Elvis Speaks* by McKeon, Elizabeth and Everett, Linda. Cumberland House Publishing, Tennessee. 1997.

Presley, Elvis quoted in *Last Train to Memphis* by Guralnick, Peter. Little Brown and Company, London. 1994.

Beaulieu Presley, Priscilla. *Elvis and Me.* Arrow Books, London. 1986.

Marsh, Peter & Collett, Peter. *Driving Passion: The Psychology of the Car.* Jonathan Cape. London. 1986.

Chapter 5

Presley, Elvis quoted in *Elvis Speaks* by McKeon, Elizabeth and Everett, Linda. Cumberland House Publishing, Tennessee. 1997.

Presley, Gladys quoted *The Girls' Guide to Elvis* by Adelman, Kim. Broadway Books, New York. 2002.

Cavendish, Deborah. *Wait For Me!: Memoirs of the Youngest Mitford Sister.* John Murray, London. 2011.

Kirwan-Taylor, Helen. 'Elvis's Style Is King Again' *The Wall Street Journal.* 19th June 2014.

Golden, George. 'The King and if Graceland is rotten to décor, don't blame it on Elvis' former decorator George Golden'. *Phoenix New Times Online*. (October 2001).

Lutyens, Dominic, & Hislop, Kirsty. *70s Style & Design*. Thames & Hudson, London. 2009.

Merrill, Hugh. *The Blues Route: From the Delta to California, a writer searches for America*. William Morrow, New York, 1990.

Harris, John. 'Talking About Graceland'. *The Guardian*. (27th March 2006)

Guralnick, Peter. *Careless Love: The Unmaking of Elvis Presley*. Little, Brown and Company, London. 2000.

Presley, Priscilla. 'Hollywood at Home'. *Architectural Digest*, Vol 65: Number 11, 2008.

Photo Credits

Cover, 42, 57, 58, 61, 68, 71, 101, 102, 133, 160. Photofest.

2, 26, 64, 70, 75, 78, 79, 85, 86, 91, 92, 83, 129, 148, 149, 150, 152, 179. Courtesy of Julien's Auctions.

6, 23. Alfred Wertheimer images provided by Pam Wertheimer.

9, 15, 19, 22, 25. Images from the Bernard J. Lansky Collection.

14, 41, 135. Country Music Hall of Fame® and Museum.

16, 20, 28, 30, 31, 38, 39, 88, 106, 108. The Library of Congress.

24, 27, 37, 39, 43, 47, 48, 51, 52, 59, 63, 64, 75, 79, 80, 81, 82, 88, 90, 94, 107, 110, 136, 167, 171, 172, 180, 182, 185, 186. Images courtesy of Heritage Auctions, HA.com.

32. Product images courtesy of Sean O'Neal. Montage by Xanda. net

39. Paul Fraser Collectibles.

45, 77, 99, Photographs courtesy of Hard Rock Cafe International (USA), Inc. All rights reserved.

53. Bonhams.

55, 56. Alfred Shaheen images courtesy of Camille Shaheen.

76, 87, 95, 99. Photos courtesy of Keith Alverson.

71. Leslie Hindman Auctioneers.

96. © Photo by Masayoshi Sukita.

105, 106. Copyright - J. Strickland & Co.

115, 126, 192, 193, 194, 196, 198. Photographs from the Carol M. Highsmith Archive, Library of Congress, Prints and Photographs Division.

127. Image provided courtesy of ElvisKarate.com.

130, 154, 170. Shutterstock.

140. Photos provided by Buck Owens Private Foundation.

141. Photos provided by the National Automobile Museum.

142. Photos provided by the Volo Auto Museum.

144. Photos provided by the Petersen Automotive Museum.

145. Image courtesy of Sue and Steve Horn and the National Motor Museum, Beaulieu.

147. Image courtesy of the Elvis Presley Mobile Museum.

175, 185. Photos by Andrea Zucker, courtesy of Elvis Presley Enterprises.

Acknowledgments

My sincere gratitude to all the fashion and design experts who agreed to be interviewed for *Elvis Style* – your opinions are highly prized. Thank you to Graceland Randers museum in Denmark, who threw open their doors and let me delve in and document their collection. I am grateful to all the collectors, auction houses and photographers who have kindly provided images for publication. A special thank you to Eric Bradley, public relations associate at Heritage Auctions and author of the wonderful book *Mantiques: A Manly Guide to Cool Stuff*, for his generous cooperation.

It was my pleasure to spend time with Hal Lansky at the Lansky Bros. store in Memphis, a historic site for Elvis fans and those with an interest in fashion. I am honoured that Hal, who is so closely associated with Elvis' dress, has provided the foreword for *Elvis Style*.

Index